Parables for a Wounded Heart

Overcoming the Wounds to Your Self-Esteem and Transforming Your Perception of You

Terry L. Ledford, Ph.D.

ISBN: 0-6156-6921-2
ISBN-13: 9780615669212

Dedication

This book is dedicated to those who have made my life brighter and encouraged me along the way: my wife Sheila, my children Chuck, Christy and Suzanne, my children-in-law Eric and Brandy, and my grandchildren, Alex, Avery, Payton, Parker, Madison, the one on the way and any more that will come along-my blessings!

Table of Contents

Index to the Parables

Acknowledgements

This book wasn't created. It evolved, and many people helped greatly in that process. Each person came along at exactly the right time. Isn't it amazing how that seems to work?

First, I want to thank my wife of thirty-eight years, Sheila. You began boosting my self-esteem when I was only sixteen and haven't stopped since. You have encouraged me in every step of my career (and life) and you continued with this project. Thank you for everything!

A big thank you to my parents, Talmadge and Joan, who created a home where I felt safe, loved and competent. You told me that I could do anything I wanted to do until I believed it. Thank you Suzanne, my youngest daughter and a great counselor in your own right. Your comments, encouragement and suggestions have meant a lot. Thank you to Melody Urban, M.A. who, as an intern, urged me to write my therapeutic stories down until I finally did.

My sincere thanks to my editor, Marc Haeringer. Marc, you helped me turn a collection of therapeutic stories and exercises into a treatment presentation. Not only did I agree with your suggestions, they rang so true that I couldn't believe I hadn't already thought of them.

Thank you to all those who read the various versions of the manuscript and offered your edits and suggestions. Your time, thoughts and expertise were wonderful. For your contributions I thank Pat Snyder, Gene Wilson, Ph.D., Mack McKeithan, Sara Kirk, Rose Bass, Richard Bass, Jack Culbreth, M.A., L.C.A.S., and John Miracle, M.A. and again, Sheila.

Finally, I want to thank the many clients who have honored me with their trust through the last thirty years. I have said before that most of what I know, I learned from my clients. This is especially true for the concepts described in this book. Thank you for allowing me to share in your journey.

Introduction

Imagine a hospital nursery. You stand in the hall and gaze through the window at a room full of newborn babies. They lie in acrylic trays wrapped in pink or blue blankets. Some are asleep; others are crying. These babies are all precious and loveable. They are all important and deserve attention and care. They are equally valuable.

However, in twenty-four to forty-eight hours, each baby will leave this nursery and will be taken home. Some will go to homes where they are loved and treasured. Some will go to homes where they are unwanted, ignored and rejected. Some will be given attention and patience, as they are taught new skills. Those children will receive reassurance and encouragement when they fail. Other children will be criticized or put down when they make the mistakes that all children make.

The babies aren't different. The homes are different. The treatment the baby receives depends on the nature of the caregivers, not the worth of the baby. The baby doesn't know this. A wound of the heart occurs.

For the past thirty years, I have been providing psychotherapy in private practice. In those years, I have seen so many people who suffer from wounds of the heart, people who live their lives with negative beliefs about themselves, beliefs that cause them to hurt deeply. Those people usually don't appear to be hurting on the outside. They go to work, raise children, and belong to churches or other community organizations. Sometimes, they are very successful on the outside. Some may be professionals, owners of businesses, or helpers themselves. Most people show no outward signs of the emotional pain they are experiencing inside, yet they do experience that pain. Many people judge themselves internally and feel they are different from others. They fear that others will soon discover their inadequacies.

My psychotherapy practice has been very busy for many years. Through these years I have been blessed to be able to be to see many clients heal their wounds of the heart and to be a part of that change. I discovered long ago that my purpose here on this earth is to touch other people in such a way that they can grow, learn and heal. That is also the reason I have written this book. My hope is that these pages will touch you in a way that brings about healing.

More specifically, I have written this book to help you gain an accurate perception of a most important subject—- YOU. While this book does provide more information, that is not what it is about. Many other books do that quite nicely. This book is about giving you a different way of seeing yourself, a more accurate perception of yourself. The stories are designed to help you look at yourself in a new way. When we see ourselves in a new way we can change our lives.

As we begin this journey together, I want you to know that I have a tremendous respect for you. You are willing to look deeper, to question your assumptions and your perceptions, and to initiate change. If you will commit to the steps outlined in this book, you will change your life. The journey begins.

Terry L. Ledford, Ph.D.

Chapter 1
Assessing the Wound and the Cure

All psychological problems, from the slightest neurosis to the deepest psychosis, are merely symptoms of the frustration of the fundamental need for a sense of personal worth. Self-esteem is the basic element in the health of any human personality.
Dr. William Glasser,
Founder of William Glasser Institute

Do you believe that you are smart or not smart, attractive or unattractive, likeable or not likeable, interesting or boring, a good person or a bad person? What are your beliefs about who you are?

Your answers to these questions determine whether you will be happy or unhappy, successful or unsuccessful. Your answers affect everything.

We begin forming the answers to these questions very early in childhood. The child forms the answers by listening to the messages given by parents, step-parents, grandparents, teachers and peers. The first and most powerful messages come from the child's parents or primary caretakers.

Some children are born to parents who are loving, stable and encouraging. Those parents provide limits yet foster the child's independence. Through their behaviors those parents give their children messages that they are lovable and competent. Their children believe those positive messages. They develop positive beliefs about themselves.

Other children are born to parents who are critical, harsh, neglectful, or abandoning. Some of those parents are even abusive. Those parents give their children messages that they are defective, inadequate or unimportant. Their children believe those negative messages as well. They develop negative beliefs about themselves.

The negative messages wound the child. The wound is deep. The wound alters the child's sense of self. The wound strikes at the child's core. The child thus sustains a wounded heart.

A wound of the heart is a hurt or a series of hurts that affects your core being, sense of self or self-concept. The wounded heart alters your perception of yourself, of the world, or of how you fit or do not fit into the world. Such a wound tends to redefine your identity—not who you are but who you believe you are.

Most of the time, we hide a wound of the heart. We try very hard to present an acceptable façade to the world. We smile. We try to interact in all the socially acceptable ways. Our outward appearance rarely betrays the wound within.

Many times a wound of the heart is also hidden from the one who is wounded. Oh, they know they have been hurt at some time in the recent or the distant past, but they often don't realize the impact of that hurt on every aspect of their life. They live their lives unconsciously responding to the painful directives of the wound.

You see, a wound of the heart doesn't just sit there passively causing pain. This type of wound guides your thinking, alters your perceptions and affects your life choices. It changes your life, and you don't even know that it is happening. A wounded heart can destroy a life if left untreated.

While a wound of the heart can occur at any age, most wounds occur during childhood when the heart is young and most tender. The child is most vulnerable because the sense of self is just forming, and he or she has no defense against such a wound. From the moment the child is able to recognize that he is a distinct being, separate from the world, he begins gathering information to answer that question, "Who am I?"

Many times an early wound can predispose the person to make choices that set the stage for later wounds to occur. The woman abused during childhood marries the man who later becomes abusive. The man who was told that he would never succeed unconsciously sabotages himself whenever he is close to success. The college student drops out of college after the first failure experience. The single woman doesn't initiate social activities because she believes others are too busy for her. They are unaware that their adult experiences are the direct result of the childhood wound of the heart. Each choice creates circumstances that serve to greatly deepen that wound.

My goal in this book is to help you recognize any wounds of the heart you may have sustained, to stop those wounds from causing further damage, and to initiate healing. The process presented here worked for many of my clients, and it can work for you. You don't have to continue living with the pain of those wounds. Others have experienced healing from heart wounds, and so can you.

The healing process presented in this book combines the proven principles of Cognitive Therapy with the emotional power of therapeutic stories. Cognitive Therapy appeals to the intellectual mind while stories appeal to the emotional mind. This combination will facilitate a deep and lasting healing for your heart wound.

Using Cognitive Therapy:

In Cognitive Therapy we examine the beliefs that were taught by your childhood (and later) events. We then look at the thoughts that tend to pop into your head, as you go through your day. The goal of the therapy is to alter any inaccurate, self-destructive beliefs and help the client break the habit of self-critical, negative thinking. Cognitive Therapy works to help the client replace false, negative thinking with more accurate or factual thinking.

The term used in Cognitive Therapy for our cluster of beliefs about ourselves and the world is "schema." The literal meaning of "schema" is a set of defining beliefs or characteristics for anything. For example, your schema for "dog" may include four legs, fur, tail, barking sounds, etc. We formed our schema for a dog from our prior experiences with dogs.

We would actually have a hard time living without schema because we would have to process everything we encounter as if we were seeing it for the first time. Because of our schema we can identify an object as a dog without having to think about it.

The schema idea goes beyond simple identification of an object. It also defines our expectations for that object. For example, our schema for "dog" determines what we expect from a dog. We develop our expectations for a dog from our actual experiences with dogs and from the things we have been told about dogs. If our parents have warned us that dogs are dangerous and will bite us, we will have expectations that all dogs will hurt us. We will also interpret a dog's behavior to suggest danger even when it just wants to play. If we encounter a dog that is obviously friendly, we may perceive that dog as an "exception to the rule," which allows our belief that dogs are dangerous to remain unchanged. Since we believe dogs to be dangerous we will avoid any extended contact, thus reducing the possibility of our having positive experiences with friendly dogs that might disprove our belief. We maintain our belief that dogs are dangerous because the belief alters our expectations, perceptions and behaviors.

What does all this talk about dogs have to do with you? Your schema about yourself works the same way. Your beliefs about yourself are resistant to change because those beliefs alter your expectations, perceptions, and behaviors. You pay attention and accept those events that seem to confirm your prior beliefs about you while discounting those experiences that refute your beliefs.

Our brains use several processes to maintain our existing beliefs or schema. I call these processes "Belief Keepers" because their sole purpose is to keep our existing beliefs from being changed or altered. As you read about each Belief Keeper, consider whether you have been using that process to hold on to your negative beliefs about yourself.

Perceptual Distortion:
There are two types of perceptual distortions-mind reading and selective attention.

a. Mind Reading: This is when you assume you know what someone is thinking or feeling about you. Of course, you can't actually read people's minds, but you assume and feel quite certain that you know what they are thinking or feeling. Your assumptions will always be consistent with your learned negative beliefs. For example, if you learned to believe that you are inadequate or incompetent, you will always make mind reading assumptions that others are thinking critical or disapproving thoughts about you or your work. You will never assume that others are thinking positive things about you.

b. Selective Attention: This is when you pay attention to certain experiences while ignoring other experiences. You always pay attention to the events that agree with your beliefs while ignoring those experiences that are inconsistent with your beliefs.

The Exclusion Delusion:

This occurs when you apply one set of rules to all other human beings, but believe that you are an exception to that rule. For example, you fully believe that no child deserves to be sexually abused, but you believe that you must have done something to deserve the abuse you experienced as a child.

Emotional Compass:

Emotional Compass occurs when you listen to your feelings as a guide of the truth. Your feelings will always be consistent with your self-beliefs even when those beliefs are totally inaccurate. For instance, you may intellectually know that a failure event wasn't your fault but you still feel that it was. You listen to that feeling and react as if the event was your fault.

Blame Magnet:

This is when you blame yourself for anything bad that happens to you or to those around you. You will sometimes rationalize a reason the event is your fault; but sometimes you persist in believing it was your fault, even without any rationalization.

You will find more information on the Belief Keepers in Appendix A (page 201). As you continue the work in this book, notice how often your mind uses the Belief Keepers to maintain your negative beliefs about yourself.

Using Parables or Stories:

During counseling, I frequently address my client's wounds of the heart by using therapeutic stories or metaphors. I like using stories in my practice for several reasons. First, they seem to have been effective as teaching tools through the ages. Every culture has had its storytellers, who carried forward their shared experience by telling tales. Second, stories suggest movement and change. A story has a beginning, middle, and an end. Things change. People change. Outcomes change within the story. Third, we tend to form an emotional connection to the characters in a story, particularly when that character is experiencing something we have felt but never shared. Finally, when we learn through stories we are free to take the truths from the story that most pertain to us and apply them as we need for our own personal growth.

The moral or point of each story is straightforward and simple. The stories themselves are simple and sometimes childlike. This was intentional. They were constructed to strike a chord with the wounded child within.

I use therapeutic stories or parables in this book just as I do in my practice. Each story is designed to teach particular truths. People sometimes ask me if certain stories are true. Some are true in that they did actually happen. Some didn't actually happen, but that doesn't make them any less true. Only you can judge the truth of a story for you. If the story resonates within you, you will know it, and it will be true for you.

Purpose, Perception and Persistence:

As you work through this book, you will be introduced to the three major components of healing your heart wounds. I have helped my clients understand these elements, and they utilized them to achieve healing of their wounds of the heart. These essential elements of healing a wound of the heart are (a) establishing a clear and intentional Purpose, (b) understanding and mastering your Perception, and (c) discovering the tools you need for Persistence. This book is divided into three parts corresponding to these steps. Let's look at each of those steps now.

Part 1: Purpose:

Healing your wound of the heart or changing your self-esteem is much like any other project you might undertake. Such healing requires a deliberate intention, energy, and hard work. If you want to build a house you pick out the house plans, find a location, and hire workers to help you. You expect to put in time, hard work, and energy until you complete the house. You establish a goal and then follow through until you complete that goal. You understand that the project is going to take some time. The same holds true for any undertaking such as taking a trip, planting a garden, or getting a college degree. In each case you establish a goal and develop a plan to achieve that goal. The goal must be important enough to motivate you and justify the time and energy required. You then have to maintain that motivation and intention until you complete the goal. Healing your wound of the heart or changing your perception of yourself is no different.

In order to heal you must first have the intention of changing your negative beliefs about yourself. You must want to destroy those negative beliefs and replace them with more positive ones. You must make it your daily intention to alter your perceptions of yourself. You must make self-esteem change your goal, your purpose. Healing your wound of the heart requires a deliberate and dedicated effort.

Many people say that they would like to feel better about themselves. Of course, no one wants to have low self-esteem, but such change is impossible without dedicated effort. To heal your heart wounds you must make the work a priority, at least in the beginning. As you gain mastery over the process the work becomes easier and easier. Then, at some point, this new way of thinking becomes second nature.

Of course, you aren't going to make it your intention to change your negative beliefs about yourself unless you first accept the possibility that those beliefs are inaccurate and harmful and that they need to be changed. This is especially difficult because they are, after all, your beliefs. You have always believed these things to be true. You may have not even questioned them until now. Even as you read these words, you may be arguing with me in your mind. Like my clients, you may be thinking that you know yourself, and you know that your negative traits are fact, not belief. I understand. Be patient and keep reading.

I fully expect that you will have great difficulty accepting the fact that your negative beliefs about yourself are untrue. They have always been a part of your reality. You feel deeply that they are true. You can probably recite a long list of life experiences that you feel confirm the accuracy of those beliefs. I will argue in later chapters that those experiences are the result of your negative beliefs, not a confirmation of them. I will demonstrate that your beliefs created the negative experiences rather than the experiences demonstrating the validity of your negative beliefs.

Let's consider the example of Nicolaus Copernicus, who lived from 1473 to 1543. Copernicus was the first person to suggest that the earth was not the center of the universe. Until then everyone believed that the sun and stars rotated around the earth. This belief was consistent with their interpretation of scripture and, they thought, was demonstrated by their daily observations. They had watched the sun and stars rise, move slowly across the sky, and set each and every day of their lives. They saw them move. They did not feel the earth move. The theory that these heavenly bodies were not moving seemed utterly ridiculous. The idea that the earth was actually moving was inconsistent with what they felt. It defied everything they had ever known. Copernicus was denounced by the church and ridiculed by many, but we now know that he was correct. The prior beliefs were wrong. Our perceptions and feelings had led us astray. All our assumptions about the universe changed with his discovery.

Does it sound a bit strong to say that changing your beliefs about yourself will actually change your universe? I don't think so. Every day of your life has been affected by your beliefs about who you are and your expectations about how the world will treat you. Your thoughts, your choices, your reactions to life events, your relationships, and your emotions are all influenced by your beliefs about who you are.

You must recognize the immense importance of this work. Otherwise, you won't make the work a priority. You won't put the intention and energy necessary to achieve success. When you understand the tremendous impact of your negative self-beliefs, you will make changing them your goal, your purpose. Only then will you begin to heal your wound of the heart. The quality of the rest of your life depends on that healing.

Part 2: Perception:

Perception is the second step in the process. Once you intellectually accept the possibility that your negative self-beliefs are inaccurate and destructive, you will begin an examination of your perceptions surrounding those beliefs.

As humans, all of our experience is determined by perception. Perception is the brain's attempt to make sense of the stimuli hitting our five senses and the mental interpretation we give to the events we experience. We may accurately perceive an event but generate an inaccurate interpretation for that event.

Most of the time, the process of perception works very well, but sometimes perception can be inaccurate. Your beliefs about yourself influence the way you perceive and interpret all the experiences of your life. Those faulty perceptions have served to maintain your wound of the heart.

You will learn to look at your negative self-beliefs in a different way. For example, when you experienced the events of your childhood, you were a child and thought and perceived as a child. Thus, you interpreted those events with a childlike understanding. As you matured your adult perspective allowed you to understand many later life events in a more realistic way, yet this more mature perspective was not applied to your childhood experience. Children are excellent recorders of events and terrible interpreters of them.

Let's consider the example of children experiencing their parent's divorce. We know that almost all children question the possibility that the divorce might have actually been their fault. They believe that their misbehaviors or defects contributed to the parental arguments or to one parent leaving. This is just one example of the fact that children tend to blame themselves for most events they experience. As adults, we understand that children don't have the power to create a divorce or to prevent one. We understand that the adults are fully responsible. Unfortunately, children don't have that perspective.

While you have gained an adult perspective for most issues, you have continued to interpret the events from your own childhood with your "child eyes." You have continued to see your childhood experiences with the incomplete understanding of a child. This is normal. We all do this.

As part of this healing, you will learn to look at your childhood experiences with your adult eyes so that you can see them more clearly. I will help you reexamine your negative childhood events with your adult understanding. You will discover a new interpretation or meaning for those experiences. Your new interpretation of the events will help you alter the beliefs you hold about yourself. This will help you heal your wound of the heart. You may have to approach a belief from a number of different angles before you can fully understand that it is false and destructive. That is normal as well.

Part 3: Persistence:

The third step in healing the heart wound is persistence. The human mind resists changing beliefs, even when those beliefs are harmful. In order to accomplish more than an intellectual change in belief, we must remind ourselves repeatedly of the truth. While we may quickly accept the truth with our heads, repetition is necessary to gain that acceptance with our heart. Then you don't just believe that it's true, you know it to be true. You will need to continually monitor your negative thinking and stop such thinking when it occurs. You will have to be persistent in your efforts to change.

There are several factors that make persistence necessary. The first is the subtle nature of our thinking. Thoughts pass through our minds quickly without conscious effort or awareness. We discover that we have been thinking about a particular topic for several minutes before we become aware that we are thinking of it at all. This is particularly destructive when the train of thought is a self-critical one. Those negative thoughts deepen the wound of the heart. You can do much damage before you even discover the fact that you are doing it.

A second factor that necessitates persistence involves the fact that you will continue to have negative experiences while you are doing this work. I have commented before that I could do great therapy if the client's life didn't get in the way. Clients will be making good progress, and then between sessions some hurtful event will occur that sets them back. Such setbacks are also normal. When they occur you just have to continue the process of healing and not give up.

Your wound of the heart has influenced your life choices and impacted your relationships and behaviors. By this time you probably have relationships with some people who reinforce the negative opinions you have about yourself. These relationships could be with a spouse, friends or co-workers. These people may be critical, disapproving, or rejecting. While you are working hard to develop an improved, more factual, image of yourself they may seem to be working just as hard to keep you from changing. This may be intentional or unintentional. These hurtful relationships may be those you established in adulthood, or they may be continued interactions with hurtful parental figures.

You must persist because you are still dealing with choices or behaviors you made because of your heart wound and you now consider them inappropriate or immoral. You may be dealing with the guilt of inappropriate behaviors. Perhaps you are unhappy in a dead-end job because you chose to drop out of school. You could be overwhelmed by multiple responsibilities because you were unable to assertively say no. Because of past choices your daily circumstances may seem to be shouting those same old negative belief statements regarding who you are or how the world will treat you.

Finally, you will need persistence to combat your brain's natural tendency to maintain existing beliefs. Those Belief Keepers discussed above are continually and vigilantly working to maintain your prior beliefs. You will need to watch for a tendency to do Mind Reading, Selective Perception, Exclusion Delusion, Emotional Compass and Blame Magnet.

In Part 3, I will help you develop a set of tools to persistently challenge your negative self-beliefs and establish a routine to apply those tools on a daily basis. You will need to utilize those tools long after you have finished this book.

How to Use This Book:

This book is meant to be used as a manual, not read cover-to-cover like a novel. You will encounter homework exercises at the end of each chapter. I ask that you complete the homework as it applies to your life experience. Some homework assignments require you to write down responses and some require thought exercises.

In counseling I usually ask the client to do homework between sessions and bring it in to the next session. Without homework the client just benefits from the hour. With homework the client can continue working all week. Your homework will be to complete the exercises provided at the end of the stories. Please take the time to do each exercise before you move on to the next section. Otherwise, you will gain very little.

Each chapter will conclude with some comments that I might make to a client at the conclusion of a counseling session. The comments will address the homework and some of the responses other clients have had to that homework. The comments are also intended to encourage and support you as you proceed through this journey. It's not an easy journey, and I recognize that.

If you connect with a story, read it more than once. The meaning of the story may become deeper for you with each reading. Allow yourself to take the time to ponder its meaning for you and your experience. Read it with your heart, not just with your head.

The stories are simple and straight-forward. Parables are usually simple. Sometimes the simplest ideas are the most profound. The difficulty with a parable is not understanding its truth but applying its truth to our lives. The work of this book is applying the truths of the stories to your life, to your heart.

The stories in this book are presented in a particular order. This would generally be the order that I would share the stories if working with a client in my practice. Later stories are told with the assumption that the client had already been introduced to ideas presented in earlier stories, so it is my recommendation that you read the stories in the order presented and that you complete the exercises at the end of one story before you go on to the next.

You will note that some of the chapters use the female gender and some use the male gender. I believe this is less awkward than using he/she throughout. The therapeutic messages conveyed by each story apply equally to males and females.

You might find it helpful to give yourself a week to work on the homework and ponder the story before moving on to the next chapter. This will make the experience more similar to an actual counseling experience. However, you may need to take breaks from the book at times. The stories are designed to help you heal your childhood wounds, but to do that you have to remember the events that created those wounds. If you begin to feel overwhelmed, depressed or irritable, you may need to take a break from the work or seek professional counseling. This book can also be used as part of your counseling experience if the counselor agrees.

This book should not be considered a substitute for professional counseling. If you are experiencing significant difficulties, get the help of a professional therapist, but be careful in choosing a counselor. I have found that many counselors are of little benefit, and some are downright dangerous. If you feel you aren't benefiting from your counseling, tell the therapist your concerns. If the counseling doesn't improve, seek another counselor.

Chapter 2
Addressing Resistance to Treatment

You cannot expect to achieve new goals or move beyond your present circumstances unless you change.
Les Brown

At this point, I anticipate that some of you may be having questions or objections to what you're reading. At least such is true with many of my clients when I explain this treatment program. These objections are normal. They are simply part of the healing process. I have addressed some common objections or questions below. If your concern isn't addressed here, it should come up in later chapters. Here are some of the concerns commonly expressed by my clients.

1.   <u>I'm too old. I've been this way too long. I can't change now.</u>
This is a common objection, and I understand the reasoning. The argument makes sense. It just doesn't seem to be true. I have found that my older clients are able to do this work as effectively as my younger clients. Some of my older clients have even changed more quickly than clients half their age. The determining factor seems to be the willingness to make some important decisions. The decision to honestly entertain the possibility that previous thoughts and beliefs were inaccurate is crucial. This is followed by the decision to make healing their purpose, their priority. Sometimes I think that older clients have the advantage of their many years of experiencing the damage caused by their negative beliefs. They understand, more than younger individuals, the immense importance of this work. This increases their motivation to rid themselves of such thoughts.

Whatever the reason, age doesn't seem to be a factor. Yes, you can change.

2. **My adult life experiences, my failures, mistakes or rejections, confirm my negative beliefs about myself.**

As I stated earlier, your negative life experiences do confirm something, but not the validity of your negative beliefs. Your negative self-beliefs (or your wound of the heart) have significantly influenced your life choices and perceptions of events. Your negative adult life experiences were a result of your negative self-beliefs, not a confirmation of them. As you work through the section on Perception, you will learn to see those adult failures in a very different way. The meaning of those experiences will become clear to you. For now, be patient.

3. **I should be over my childhood stuff by now. Am I just weak?**

Without some type of intervention, wounds of the heart sustained during childhood are permanent. This is true for every human being. As you will see in Chapter 3, our minds process such events in a way that maintains and sometimes strengthens, their impact. The length of time that has passed since the events occurred is not relevant.

4. **My childhood wasn't all that bad.**

Sometimes, people recognize that they feel negatively about themselves, but they resist connecting that negative self-opinion to their childhood experience. They believe that their negative opinions of themselves are warranted due to their inadequacies or failures. They may tend to believe that their childhood experience was "not all that bad," or that the experience didn't have a big impact on them.

When my clients voice that opinion I ask them to imagine that their own children had to experience the exact same childhood events that they experienced. I ask them how much they think such an experience would affect their child's self-concept, attitude about life, and life choices.

Try that right now. Think about your childhood experience. Imagine that your child was made to experience those same events that happened to you. Imagine your childhood was imposed upon your child. How would you feel about that? How do you think those experiences would affect your child? Would they wound him or her? Would they alter the child's life choices? Would they damage the self-esteem? If you think your childhood experiences would have a significant impact on your child, then they probably had a significant impact on you. Remember, you were also just a child at the time. We'll deal with this issue in depth in chapter 4.

I'm not suggesting that your childhood had to be horrible. My clients' childhood experiences range from good, loving parents and a fairly stable home life to repeated, horrific abuse that would be unimaginable to most people. Some clients had fairly good experiences at home, but still developed negative beliefs about themselves because of the negative behaviors of other children, teachers, spouses, or others outside the family. Some were impacted by a parent's death during childhood or by a serious childhood illness. Others didn't acquire a serious wound of the heart until adulthood.

5.   <u>Some people had it so much worse than me.</u>

There isn't a perfect correlation between the negativity of the childhood experience and the negativity of self-esteem. Sometimes many small insults to the self can equal the impact of one major abusive event. I generally discourage my clients from trying to make comparisons to other people's wounds or the impact of those wounds. They will sometimes feel guilty for needing help when others "had it so much worse than I." Their words remind me of the old saying, "I complained that I had no shoes until I met a man who had no feet." My thought is that his having no feet doesn't keep your feet from getting cold without shoes. If the wound is impacting your life, reminding yourself that others had it worse doesn't heal the wound. It may just keep you from addressing it.

6.   **I don't want to excuse current bad behaviors because of a "bad" childhood.**

I totally agree. While childhood wounds of the heart do have a lasting impact, they shouldn't be used as an excuse for inappropriate or hurtful current behaviors. Regardless of the wounds we may have acquired, we are 100% responsible for our current choices and actions. Many people attempt to excuse negative, hurtful behaviors by asserting that they aren't responsible since they experienced bad childhood events. I disagree with this reasoning.

At the same time, it is important to understand the factors that contributed to our mistakes or bad behaviors. As you proceed in this work, you will learn to address your mistakes with the same compassion you would offer to others while still taking full responsibility for your actions.

Also, this book is about healing wounds of the heart, not obsessing about them. We have to examine the wounds in order to understand them and their impact on our lives. Once we understand the nature of the wounds and correct their impact on our beliefs and perceptions, we can allow them to fade into the background of the past, and move on with our lives. Obsessing about past hurts will simply keep the heart wound open and bleeding.

7.   **I'm afraid that this work will create negative feelings toward my parents/family, and I love them.**

It is true that recalling negative experiences perpetrated by parents or family members can bring out feelings of anger toward them. It is not my intent to make you feel negatively about your family. It is my intent to help you heal your heart wounds, and doing so will require that you acknowledge the truth. To heal your heart wounds, you must recognize the truth of your experience.

You can acknowledge the hurtful behavior while continuing to love the person. Consider the life experience of the offending family member. Did they experience negative events in their childhood? Were they abused or neglected? While a negative background does not excuse inappropriate current behaviors (see item 6 above), it can help you be more compassionate and forgiving toward the person.

You don't have to confront your parents or alienate them as a result of this work. You will still have the freedom to choose the relationship you desire with your family members.

8. **If I let up on myself, I'm afraid I will stop trying at all and become a complete loser!**

As you will discover in Chapter 9, this reasoning is faulty. You will also discover that you wouldn't apply the reasoning to anyone else. I have never seen this fear realized, and I don't expect to. Actually, the opposite happens. When you feel better about yourself, your performance improves significantly. The faulty logic of this objection is illustrated in the comic poster that states, "In this company, the beatings will continue until morale improves."

Part 1:
Purpose

In Part 1, I will help you recognize the nature of your heart wounds, that those wounds are based on earlier negative experiences, that those wounds can be healed, and the importance of that healing. In this section, we will answer the following questions:

1. What are my negative self-beliefs?
2. Where did those beliefs come from?
3. How important were my childhood negative events?
4. Would others have reacted the same way to those same events?
5. What is the truth about who I am?
6. What was the impact of my negative self-beliefs on my life?
7. How important is it that I change these beliefs? Why does it matter?

By the end of this section, I hope that you will have an understanding of the truth about you and that you will have a burning desire to heal your wounds of the heart. In Part 1, you will be introduced to a little girl, two evil researchers, an abandoned violin and an eccentric inventor; they will guide you through the healing process. Each character is waiting with a message for you. In their own way, they will guide you toward a new way of thinking about yourself and your life. Open your mind, listen to your heart, and let the healing begin!

Chapter 3
The Origins of Self-Esteem Wounds

The most important things ever said to us are said by our inner selves.
Adelaide Bry

Why does one person believe that he is smart, competent and capable, while another believes that she is inadequate, incompetent and destined to fail? Why does one person believe that she is likeable and loveable, while another believes he is boring, odd, unimportant or likely to be rejected?

Your beliefs about who you are will greatly influence your decision-making. If you believe you are competent and capable, you will be more likely to go after your dreams or desires. Your decision making will focus more on whether you want or do not want to do something, not on whether you can or cannot do it. You will be more likely to assume that you can do whatever you want to do.

Also, when you believe you are competent and capable you are less vulnerable to the inevitable failures in life. You aren't as likely to be crushed by criticism, nullified by the naysayers, or mangled by your mistakes. You see a poor performance as an exception to who you are rather than a definition of who you are. You move on and try again.

When you believe you are likeable and loveable, you approach social situations with more self-confidence. You enter relationships with an assumption that the other person will like you. You expect, and even demand, that others offer you the same respect and courtesy that you give them.

When you believe you are likeable and loveable, you are less likely to be crushed by the times when others treat you badly or ignore you completely. When someone acts distant or unfriendly, you tend to attribute the behavior to some factor in that person rather than assuming that they treated you that way because of some defective factor in you.

Self-esteem can be divided into two types, person-based self-esteem and performance-based self-esteem. Some people base their self-esteem on other's opinions of them. Are they liked or loved? Are they important to others? Do their opinions matter to others? Other people base their self-esteem on their abilities to perform. Are they smart enough? Are they successful enough? Do they receive approval or disapproval?

Heart wounds can be roughly categorized in the same way, as "person wounds" and "performance wounds." A person wound occurs when the individual is exposed to a parent/caretaker who is distant, unavailable or unaffectionate. Those behaviors convey to children that they are not important or loveable and that there is something wrong with them. People with person wounds have negative thoughts such as:

- They won't like me.
- He/she doesn't care about me.
- My feelings/opinions don't matter.
- I'm not important.
- I'm just destined to be alone.
- I'm afraid he/she will leave me.

A performance wound occurs when the individual is exposed to a parent/caretaker who is critical, judgmental or difficult to please. Those behaviors convey the message that the child is inadequate or incompetent. That child concludes that there is something wrong with his performance. People with performance wounds have negative thoughts such as:

- I can't do anything right.
- I'm not smart enough to do that.
- I can't do enough to please them.

- I wish I was as talented as she.
- I'm always messing things up.
- I can't do that.

More examples of thoughts stemming from each of these categories of wounds can be found in Appendix B on page 205. Review that list of negative self-statements and note those you use most frequently. Such statements reflect the negative beliefs that a person holds about himself or herself. Think about the statements you make in your mind. What beliefs do your statements reflect? Are your negative self-statements more often in the person category or the performance category? You will probably have some statements in both categories, but usually there are more in one area, or those in one category tend to hurt you more deeply.

I once treated a young woman named Kate who had been referred to me by her family physician. The physician had tried to treat Kate's depression with an antidepressant medication, but it wasn't working. When I called her in from the waiting room on the day of her appointment, she looked as though she had been crying. She also looked extremely tired. When we settled into my office she reported that she had been depressed as long as she could remember. She was thirty-two years old and was divorced with two children. She was a CPA with a fairly busy accounting practice.

As she described her situation her report was punctuated with self-critical comments and new tears. She said that she couldn't figure out why she couldn't "just get it together." She said that she had "obviously failed as a wife" since her husband had left her for another woman. She added that her accounting practice was doing fairly well so far, but that she always second-guessed her work and expected clients to leave her at any time. She felt as if she really wasn't smart enough to be an accountant and she would be found out eventually.

When I asked Kate about her childhood, she responded that her parents did a good job of taking care of her; but she added that her mother was very strict and never seemed to be pleased with Kate. She noted that, according to Mom, her grades were never good enough and her appearance was always lacking. When she talked about her mother it seemed as though she was transformed into that hurt little girl again. It became clear that those long-ago hurts were still very present in her life.

As she continued, Kate began to cry more openly. She recalled through her tears that her mother once told her to never let anyone see her cry. Her mother actually told her daughter that most girls look sweet when they cry, but Kate looked ugly when she cried. Kate vividly recalled that moment, noting that she had always worked very hard to hold back her tears. She couldn't hold them back that day in my office.

After gaining her composure, Kate sighed and commented quietly, "I guess she was just trying to help me. I wish somebody could." Finally she concluded, "I get so mad at myself. Sometimes, I just hate myself. I can't do anything right." When she spoke those words, her face became drawn and angry. Her shoulders stiffened and her hands became fists. The intensity of her anger toward herself became painfully obvious.

I easily felt compassion for Kate. Her mother's harsh criticism had wounded her self-esteem, and that wound followed her every day of her life. She had worn the heavy chain of inadequacy from the time she woke up to the time she fell asleep. Unfortunately, Kate's story is all too common.

I told Kate that I felt her self-esteem had a lot to do with her depressed mood. Her negative beliefs about herself triggered a constant flood of self-critical thoughts. Those thoughts created and maintained her painful clinical depression despite the fact that she had been taking antidepressants.

I explained that I do Cognitive Therapy, which works on helping people change the thinking patterns that cause depression. I told her that, based on the information she had provided, I believed she had several negative beliefs about herself. I then added that I wanted to tell her a story that illustrates the way I do therapy. I have a dry erase board mounted on the back of my office door and I went there to tell Kate "The Parable of the Stupid Little Girl."

The Parable of the
Stupid Little Girl

ॐॐ

Once there was a family with a mother, a father, and a little girl. Now, the little girl was a perfectly intelligent, cute, loveable little girl. The problem in this family was that the father tended to be very critical; and, in particular, he used the word "stupid" a lot. So when the little girl would spill her drink at the table, as children sometimes do, he would say something like "How could you be so stupid! Get the towel and get it up!" Or, when she tried to tie her shoes and tied them in a knot, he might say something like, "I don't see how anyone can be so stupid as to tie a knot this tight." We're going to say that his being critical of her and calling her stupid were EVENTS in her life.

EVENTS

One day this little girl was at her home. She wasn't old enough to go to school yet. Her daddy was not around. He was at work. Her mom was in the house doing something, and the little girl was outside playing with her doll. She accidently dropped her doll on the sidewalk, and it broke. What do you imagine she thought to herself when she saw that she had broken her doll? That's right. She called herself stupid. The events in her life had now made her believe she was stupid, not because she was, but because her father had been so critical and had called her stupid.

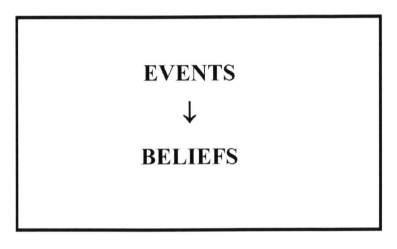

And the belief that she was stupid caused her to call herself stupid in her mind when she broke the doll. We call the words and sentences we think to ourselves "Automatic Self-Talk."

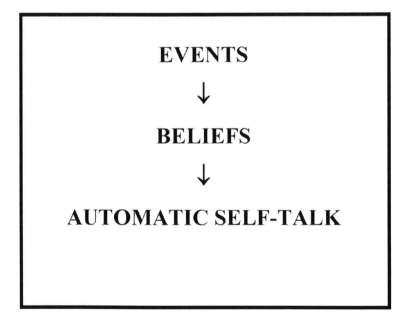

We all talk to ourselves in our minds all throughout our waking hours. From the time we wake up until the time we go to sleep we think in words and sentences. Sometimes the thoughts we think to ourselves are neutral, like "I need to get some bread on the way home." Sometimes the thoughts are positive like, "I can't wait until I get to do...." But sometimes the thoughts are negative like, "I can't believe I was so stupid!" or "I can't do anything right."

Our automatic self-talk is determined by the beliefs we have about ourselves, the world, and how we fit into the world. The thoughts we think to ourselves are a direct result of the beliefs we have learned from the prior events in our lives.

Let's look at this a little more closely. Imagine you go to a place that you visit on a regular basis. You see someone who has always been very nice to you. You say "hello" in a chipper, friendly voice; but she responds in a gruff voice, "Hello," and turns and walks away. You think to yourself, "What have I done? Why is she mad at me?"

Now, let's rewind the clock. Let's imagine that you go to this place you visit regularly. You see this person who has always been very nice to you, and you say "Hello" in your friendly, chipper voice. She says "Hello" in a gruff voice and walks away like before. But, this time you think to yourself, "Oh, I wonder if she is okay. I wonder if something happened at home!" The emotional response this time is very different from before. Your emotional response is determined more by the thought or "self-talk" that pops into your head rather than the event itself.

If events in your life have made you believe that people tend to get mad at you for no apparent reason, you will think, "Why is she mad at me?" If your earlier events made you believe that others aren't going to get mad at you unless you do something to them, you will be more likely to think, "I wonder if they are okay."

The real power of our self-talk is in the fact that it is constant and that we rarely question it. If others say something to you, you question it. You consider whether you agree with the statement. You consider the source and their bias. But when you think something to yourself, you rarely question it at all. You simply assume that it is factual.

Now let's return to the story of the little girl. She gets a little older and she goes to school. She gets back a paper with a failing grade. What thought do you think pops in her head? That's right. She thinks it's because she's stupid.

Another day comes, and this time she gets back a paper with a 100 grade written on it. What thought do you imagine might pop into her head when she sees the 100 grade? She might think that she's smart, but that's not likely. More likely, she will think something like, "That must have been an easy test" or "I got lucky." You see, the next step in the diagram is called "Selective Perception."

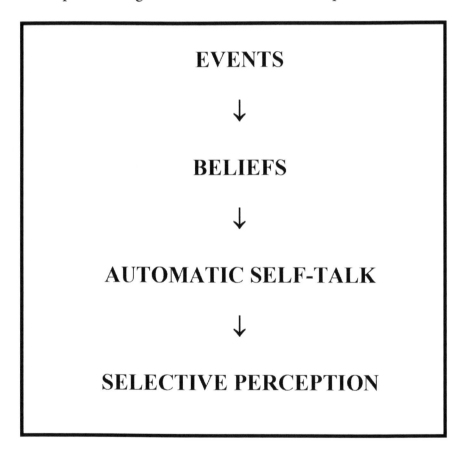

EVENTS

↓

BELIEFS

↓

AUTOMATIC SELF-TALK

↓

SELECTIVE PERCEPTION

"Selective Perception" means that we have a tendency to accept and believe only those events that go along with our existing beliefs about ourselves and the world. If I believe I am stupid, and I make a 100 grade on a test, I tend to have an automatic thought pop into my mind that explains it away. My thoughts negate the positive event; but if I have a negative event that is consistent with my belief that I am stupid, I accept the event as true, analyze it, obsess about it, and remember it forever. It then becomes another event that reinforces my original belief that I'm stupid.

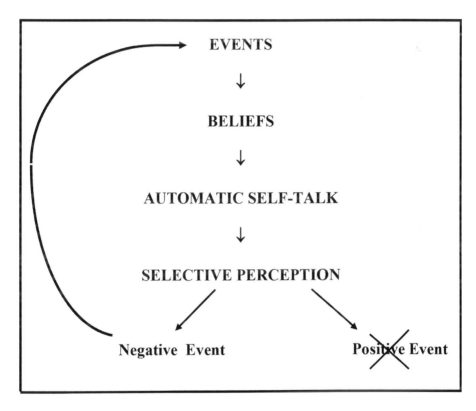

As you can see, this process can become a vicious cycle, where we maintain our negative beliefs learned during childhood, throughout life. Since we accept and pay attention only to those events that are consistent with our childhood beliefs, our later life experiences appear to confirm the early negative beliefs. Those negative early beliefs persist and even become strengthened throughout our lives.

Applying the Parable

Where do your beliefs come from? As the story illustrates, your beliefs about yourself are the result of your prior experiences and not necessarily a reflection of truth. When you were growing up, you were given messages just like the little girl in the story. You absorbed or internalized those messages and they became your self-esteem.

If you were fortunate enough to be surrounded by parents and others who communicated positive messages, then you learned to believe good things about yourself. If you were surrounded by parents or others who were critical, demanding, negative, or rejecting, then you learned to believe negative things about yourself.

It is important to remember that the messages you received included verbal and non-verbal statements. Sometimes the most damaging messages are the non-verbal ones. A look of disapproval or disgust can convey a message that you are defective and inadequate. A cold and distant demeanor or a lack of attention can create a belief that you are not important or loveable. Whether the negative messages consist of verbal statements or non-verbal behaviors, the result is a child with negative beliefs about self or a "wound of the heart."

Unfortunately, the child has no choice in whether to accept or reject a particular message. A child is like a sponge. A sponge will soak up whatever liquid it contacts. If the sponge contacts pure, clean water, it soaks up water and retains that. If the sponge contacts acid, it will soak that up and retain it as well. One sponge contains pure water, and the other contains acid. The sponges have no choice in the matter. The substance placed on the sponge makes all the difference. Children soak up whatever life gives them. They tend to retain whatever they soak up. They have no choice.

You already know this to be true. You knew that the little girl in the story would call herself stupid. You knew she did not have the understanding or the power to resist the negative messages given by her father.

Before I ever finished telling the story to Kate, she was crying openly and nodding in agreement. She asked me how I could know so much about her when we had just met. Kate said she felt sad for that little girl because she was that little girl.

In order to help Kate further incorporate the truths of the story, I asked her to write down some of the events in her life that affected her self-esteem and her beliefs that came from those events. The following homework is designed to help you identify your beliefs about yourself, the childhood events that prompted those beliefs, and the effects of those beliefs on your thoughts and your life.

I cautioned Kate that she was just beginning this process, so I didn't expect her to change her beliefs quickly. I told her that, at this point, I only asked that she entertain the possibility that her negative self-beliefs were learned but may have been untrue.

You should also realize that this is but a first step in the process of healing. Be patient with yourself. Think about the possibility that your beliefs about yourself may have come from your childhood experiences. Consider the idea that the critical or neglecting parent gave you a set of beliefs that were inaccurate and destructive. Think about the possibility that you may have been wrong in your perceptions of yourself.

Now, take the time to complete the homework before you continue reading. Let your mind go back to your childhood years. Remember what you experienced as a young girl or boy. Remember how you felt. Remember the impact of your childhood events. Remember the child that you used to be as you respond to the questions below.

A. Write down five of your childhood events that, you believe, could have had a negative effect on your self-esteem or your view of how you fit in to the world. Some of these events may have been repeated occurrences, and some may have happened only once.

1. _____

2. _____

3. _____

4. _____

5. _____

B. Write down 10 negative belief statements that could have come from those negative childhood events. The belief statements should be single sentences, written in first person. For example: "I can't do anything right" or "I'm not as important as other people." Don't worry about the Head and Heart sections for now.

Head: Heart:
% %

1. _____

2. _____

3. _____

4. _____

5. _____

6. _____

7. _____

8. _____

9. _____

10. _____

C. Monitor your thinking as you go through your week. Pay attention to the things you say to yourself in your mind. Particularly, notice any negative thoughts that bring down your self-esteem or make you feel depressed or anxious. Write some of these statements below. Don't clean them up. Write them down exactly the way you say them in your head.

1. _____

2. _____

3. _____

4. _____

5. _____

6. _____

7. _____

8. _____

9. _____

10. _____

Compare the three lists and notice that they connect in the same way they did in the story of the little girl. Your negative self-talk will be a direct result of your negative beliefs, and your negative beliefs will be a direct result of the events you experienced.

Go back and read the events you described in Part A. Consider how those events would make any child feel. Remember that you experienced those events with the understanding of a little child. You were a child. How would those events make any child feel?

Now read the belief statements you reported in Part B. Do they reflect how you tend to feel about yourself today? You may intellectually know that some of the beliefs are inaccurate but still feel them to be true in your heart. Go back now and rate the percentage to which you believe each of the belief statements. Under the word "Head" put the percentage to which you believe each statement to be true intellectually. What does your logical mind tell you? After providing a rating for all the beliefs with your head, go back and rate each belief as to the percentage to which you tend to feel that it is true in your heart, or the Heart rating. The difference in the two percentage ratings indicates that you actually know that a particular belief is wrong or inaccurate, but you still feel it to be true with your emotional self. Knowing intellectually that a belief is wrong doesn't protect you from the belief's destructive affect. Consider how living every day of your life with such beliefs has impacted you.

Now think about how you would feel if a good friend (or even a stranger) reported having the same beliefs about himself or herself? Would you believe those statements to be true about your friend? Would you want to argue with the friend about those statements?

How would you feel if your children shared that they held those self-beliefs? What would you want to do about it? How much energy would you put into helping your child change those self-beliefs? Would you make it your "purpose" to help your child heal those wounds? Why should you do any less for yourself?

Finally, read the self-talk statements you recorded in Part C. Remember that you probably think those statements all through your day. Their impact on your self-esteem is like water torture where you have to endure a constant drip of water on your forehead. Each drop is minor, but the continuous dripping becomes thunderous and can drive you insane. It's the repetition of the negative thoughts that does the damage.

D. I also recommend that you begin a journal today which you will keep as you go through this book. You can copy and use the journal form found in Appendix C on page 209 if you like. Appendix C also includes instructions for using the structured form. I would recommend the structured journal if you want to get maximum benefit from your work. If you don't want to make copies of the form, however, you can use any notebook. In the notebook put down the date each day and write about your experience. You can put down events, but be sure to record any thoughts you noticed that could negatively affect your self-esteem. Try to connect your negative thoughts to the day's events. You may find that some thoughts are so pervasive that they don't need to be triggered by an immediate event. Note those thoughts as well. As you examine your thoughts, compare their content with those noted in Part C above. Then look at how they relate to your childhood beliefs in Part B.

E. Today, begin a thought-stopping tool called the rubber band technique. A form of this tool has been used for years to help individuals rid themselves of destructive automatic self-talk. It is very simple, but surprisingly effective. An explanation of the technique can be found in Appendix D on Page 213.

Again, work on this homework for the next week before you go on to the next chapter. Try to do the journal and the rubber band technique every day until you complete the entire book. Many people find that it helps to use those tools long after they complete therapy with me.

Concluding Comments:
The simple truths presented by the "stupid" little girl are the core of this book. The idea that your negative beliefs about yourself

were learned, but may not be true, is central to any efforts to heal the self-esteem. Making the connection between your current beliefs, thoughts and behaviors and your childhood experiences is essential.

The homework assignments of this chapter are the most important of this book as well. After my client completes this particular assignment, I will usually spend the next session reviewing the events reported by the client and his or her subsequent beliefs in detail. I will ask questions to make sure that I completely and accurately understand the events listed. We discuss several examples in the client's life where the beliefs have influenced choices, emotions, or behaviors. The use of this homework doesn't end there, as I often refer back to specific statements of belief as we progress through therapy.

The homework of this chapter can also be the most difficult and painful in the book. Recalling painful childhood experiences is hard. Writing them down on paper may be even harder. You may have worked very hard to not think about those experiences. The recall may bring up visual images that hurt. I'm sorry for that pain, but the healing of a wound is sometimes painful. Sometimes, I compare this process to surgery. The surgeon must produce a wound to correct the more dangerous internal wound. The pain and discomfort is followed by healing.

My clients sometimes overlook the journal assignments and rubber band technique because they seem too simple. They are simple but often powerful agents for change. Do them every day. Like my clients, you will discover their usefulness. Continue doing the journal and rubber band technique as you progress through this entire book. The insights you gain in the following chapters will be heightened by those simple techniques.

The "stupid" little girl has shared several truths. These are:

1. Your childhood (and later) events determined your beliefs about who you are.

2. Those beliefs reflect the messages you were given, not who you really are.

3. The human mind attempts to hold onto or maintain existing beliefs, even when they are untrue.

4. Your self-beliefs trigger negative statements that go through your mind each and every day.

5. Your beliefs and self-talk have had a major impact on your life.

In the next chapter, we will look at the degree of impact of your childhood events. Were they a big deal or not a big deal? Would any other child have reacted as you reacted? Would the events have had the same impact on anyone else?

Chapter 4
Taking on a Different Perspective

Emotional abuse is a debilitating heart and soul mutilation. The deepest lasting wound with any abuse is the emotional wound.
Robert Burney

I have found that my clients tend to minimize the powerful impact of their own negative childhood experiences. When they fully recognize the destructive power of those events, they make it their purpose to change the beliefs that were created by those experiences.

This chapter will help you see your childhood events in a new light. You will discover that your reactions to those events were normal. You will also recognize the enormous impact of your negative childhood experiences. The work of this chapter will help you move further toward the goal of knowing the truth with your head and with your heart.

Sometimes the distance between the head and the heart is enormous. We can know something to be true with our head, but not know it with our heart. The logic behind the story of the stupid little girl in Chapter 3 is hard to ignore. Most of my clients relate to the process revealed in the story and intuitively know that it is true. Unfortunately, simple understanding is not sufficient to heal a heart wound.

Intellectually, we know that children are innocent. We know that no child deserves to be mistreated, neglected, or abused. We know that this truth applies regardless of the problems the child may have. A child who is poor, handicapped, unattractive, or withdrawn deserves to be nurtured and not abused. We know that the little girl didn't deserve to be called stupid. We know this to be true for every child.

While we know this to be true, we don't apply the truth to ourselves. When one has sustained a wound of the heart, logic tends to be replaced with the dictates of the wound. We can say with all certainty that no child deserves to be mistreated, while maintaining that we somehow did deserve the way we were treated. We tend to believe that we must have done something to bring about the hurts we sustained, that we deserved our wound. We believe that one rule applies to all humanity with one important exception; we believe that the rule doesn't apply to us. This is what I referred to as the Exclusion Delusion.

Even after many years as a therapist, I am still amazed at the power of heart wounds to override the individual's logic in order to hold on to self-blame. As I discussed in the introduction, the human brain is programed to maintain its preconceived notions of reality, even in the face of significant conflicting evidence. In many cases this is a valuable human trait, as it gives us a sense of stability in our world, but in the case of negative childhood beliefs this tendency is most unfortunate.

I have learned that healing a wound of the heart takes time and patience. I encourage you to allow yourself that time and to be patient with yourself. Because the negative beliefs are so engrained, letting them go and accepting the truth doesn't happen without a struggle. Even if you fully understand that the negative belief was caused by an abusive or neglectful parent, even if you intellectually know that the abuse was wrong and the message inaccurate, you will struggle. You will struggle with a subtle inner voice that quietly, but strongly, repeats the childhood belief statement. As I said above, you may know in your head that the belief is a lie; but you "feel" it to be true in your heart.

Even when you know the truth, your immediate perceptions, your knee-jerk responses, your intuitive sense will be consistent with the self-critical childhood belief. Your heart will persist in believing the lie. I have often heard clients say, "I know my negative beliefs about myself aren't true, but I just feel like they are true." This is an example of the Emotional Compass.

You may also tend to minimize the impact of your childhood experience. Do you find yourself thinking, "I should be over that by now" or "If I were stronger, those things wouldn't have affected me so much?" And yet you are fully aware that the same events would have a significant impact on any other child's life.

Our tendency to minimize the impact of our childhood experience seems to persist even when we see the impact of childhood abuse on a daily basis. One client, Michael, a social worker, exemplified this tendency. Michael had worked for the local Department of Social Services, Children's Protection Division for fourteen years. He specialized in the care of abused children. Sometimes his task was to remove them from the abusive home and arrange for a foster home placement. He was very compassionate and diligent in his duties. Michael had a heart for those children and it was obvious. There was an underlying reason for his empathy.

Michael knew the pain of those children because he also had been abused. His father was an alcoholic with terrible temper problems. The most minor of offenses were often met with bruising blows or lashes with the father's belt; but like many abuse victims, Michael said the physical beatings paled in comparison to the verbal abuse. His father had many unkind names for Michael, but "worthless" seemed to be a favorite. During the beatings, when Michael would cry, his father would laugh at him and call him a baby or Mama's boy and tell him that he was weak.

As far back as Michael could remember, he had felt a deep sense of shame. He saw himself as a weak person. He was terribly critical of himself whenever he made a mistake. While never spoken out loud, he often called himself names in his mind. One of the names he frequently called himself was "worthless," and he said it without any conscious realization that he was echoing his father's voice.

Because of his work, Michael was well aware that abuse always wounds a child's self-esteem. He knew that the abuse reflected the problems of the abuser, not some defect in the child, and he had spent many hours trying to point out that fact to the children he had rescued. Michael wanted them to realize the truth about themselves and to not believe the lie conveyed by the abuser.

Michael knew the truth about his clients but he couldn't apply that truth to his own life. When I tried to help him realize the impact of his childhood abuse on his self-esteem and his tendencies toward self-criticism, he would respond that he should have been stronger. If he had been stronger the abuse wouldn't have affected him so much.

I wanted to help Michael look at his childhood abuse in a different way. I wanted to help him recognize the power of those abusive experiences and the fact that, as a child, he was helpless to resist it. He needed to apply the truth he knew so well to that little boy that he used to be. In an effort to bring home these facts, I told him "The Parable of The Psychological Experiment."

The Parable of the
Psychological Experiment

๛๛

Imagine that there were two psychologists who wanted to do an experiment. They wanted to research the impact of negative childhood events on self-esteem. They believed that the self-esteem of the adult is formed by the events that person experienced as a child. They wanted to find out if this was true.

The two psychologists went to an elementary school to begin the experiment. They observed a class of kindergarten students until they identified a little boy who was, by all of their observations, a good example of a well-adjusted, intelligent, popular, cute little boy.

You see, these psychologists were both evil psychologists, and they were going to do an evil experiment. They kidnapped this little boy and took him to another part of the country where no one would recognize him. They gave him drugs so that he wouldn't remember his real parents who loved him very much.

The psychologists hired actors and actresses to portray the boy's parents and family. Now, here's the tricky part. Somehow, these psychologists were able to use all of your childhood memories to guide the actors and actresses. I don't know how they did this, but nonetheless, they did. They had these people do exactly the same things to this child that were done to you. In essence, the child experienced your childhood. He experienced it exactly as you experienced it: every look, every behavior, and every word. They then watched to see what would happen to the little boy's self-esteem as he grew up.

What do you think they found? What do you think his self-esteem was like when he became a young adult? What beliefs did those experiences create? Would you predict that his self-esteem turned out to be a lot like yours? Do you think that he saw himself much as you see yourself?

If he experienced your childhood, exactly as you did, would he believe himself to be smart or stupid; important or unimportant;

likeable or unlikeable, adequate or inadequate? How would he see himself in relation to the world?

Remember, the psychologists chose him because he was perfectly normal. There wasn't anything wrong with him at all. He was the best in his class; but he learned to believe that there was something wrong with him, just like you did.

You will be happy to know that "the psychologist police" found out about these evil psychologists and their evil experiment. They arrested them and took them off to "psychologist jail." They certainly deserved it.

Once the psychologists were safely in jail, the police told the little boy, who was now an adult, that the whole thing was an evil experiment and that he had a wonderful family who loved him very much. They told him that there was nothing actually wrong with him. Do you think that he would believe them right away? Of course he wouldn't. He would have now experienced years of negative thoughts about himself, and would have interpreted his life events as confirmation of his inadequacy. Convincing him of the truth about himself would be like trying to tell him that the earth actually moves around the sun when he has watched the sun move across the sky every day of his life. It would take some time and a lot of work to help him learn to believe the truth.

But let's take the story a bit further. Imagine that this experiment was done with your child. He or she was the child who was kidnapped. How angry would you be? Of course, you would be infuriated. You would never want your child to be hurt in that way. You would not want your child to experience your childhood.

Applying the Parable

Your childhood experiences did have a major impact on your perceptions of yourself, and therefore your response was normal. Perhaps, you have tried to forget your childhood. You minimized the negativity of events, saying things like, "That was a long time ago." or "I'm an adult now, and I should be over that stuff by now." or "I shouldn't let that stuff bother me."

When you imagine your early life events happening to an innocent child, it's not hard to recognize their impact on the self-esteem. Michael had no trouble predicting the impact of his abuse on the child in the experiment, but he didn't seem to make an emotional connection. That is, not until he imagined that his own son, age four, was the kidnapped child. He became visibly angry at the thought that his son would have to experience his abuse. He said that he had worked very hard to not act like his father. His goal as a parent was to be the opposite of his father in every way. I knew the answer, but I asked him why he worked so hard to parent his son differently. He responded, somewhat incredulously, that it was because no child deserved to be treated that way. After his response, he smiled and said that I had tricked him. I agreed.

Michael's emotional connection to the story strengthened when I had him bring in a photo of his son along with a picture of himself as a child. During that session, I had him really look at his photo alongside the photo of his little boy. As he did this, he began to realize that he was just as innocent and just as vulnerable as his own son. After some time he began to cry. He then said, "I guess I've been abusing myself all this time, just as my father did." I knew that Michael had begun the process of healing. He still had a long way to go, but he was on his way.

As I continued to work with Michael, he used the journal and the rubber band technique discussed in Chapter 3 to increase his awareness of his self-abusive thought patterns. Some weeks brought progress and some weeks didn't. He continued to have good days and bad days, but over time, he learned to perceive himself and treat himself in a more healthy way.

After telling Michael the story of the evil experiment, I gave him the following homework. Hopefully, the work will help you apply the truth of the story to yourself.

1. Which of your childhood experiences would you <u>least</u> want visited upon the child in the experiment?

    _____

    _____

----

2.   Write six emotions or feelings the child could experience if forced to endure that event.

----

3.   Did you have those feelings when that event happened to you?

4.   Do you tend to have those same feelings now?

5.   Write down your feelings about the experiment. Write how you would feel if the experiment were carried out on your child. Note any new insights you gain about the circumstances that created your self-beliefs.

----

6.   Find some pictures of yourself as a child. Study those photos alongside pictures of your own children at the same or similar ages. Notice how small, fragile, helpless and innocent both children are. Realize the fact that neither child deserved to experience those negative events.

Now remember that those events did happen to you. Allow yourself to feel compassion for that child you used to be.

7. In this story you have been asked to put someone else in your shoes. When you imagine your childhood events happening to someone else, you should be able to see their impact more clearly. Recognizing the powerful and destructive impact of your childhood experiences should strengthen your sense of purpose in healing the heart wounds they created. Let yourself stay with this chapter until you are able to see that your reactions were completely normal, not weak or defective.

Concluding Comments:

The devastating impact of a wound of the heart is never more apparent than when a client does the activity in number six above. I have done psychotherapy for more than thirty years, but I am still amazed by the client's reactions, as they sit in my office and look at their childhood photos. There is nothing unusual about the photo. Often, it is a small school picture. I can easily see that the child is just a cute, normal child. I then hear my client saying that she doesn't like that child, or that the child is ugly. I see the looks of disapproval or even disgust on the client's face. In that moment, I clearly see the impact of the wound. In that particular moment, it is apparent that the client is out of touch with reality.

As you complete this week's homework, you may still find yourself minimizing the impact of your childhood experiences. I don't know why we do this, but most of us do. I think some people discount the impact of the experiences because recognizing the significance of the wound might change their perceptions or feelings about the one who inflicted the wound. They don't want to feel negatively about a parent or step-parent. It is not my intent to make you feel negatively about your parents or family members. It is my intent to help you stop feeling negatively about yourself!

The evil psychologists have shared several truths. These are:

1. The events of your childhood were significant.
2. Those events would have a significant impact on any other child.
3. Most children would have responded just as you did.
4. Just like the child in the experiment, you were innocent and didn't deserve the negative events you experienced.
5. The fact that you are still affected by your childhood is normal, not a sign of weakness. Not being impacted by those events would be abnormal.
6. Changing your negative beliefs will be difficult because you have now experienced years of events that you believe confirm those beliefs.
7. The work of changing your self-beliefs is enormously important. It will change the rest of your life.

Chapter 5
Learning to Love Yourself

When I grow up I want to be a little boy.
Joseph Heller

The next step in the healing process is developing an attitude of compassion toward the child you used to be. When you can look at your childhood self with compassion, you will make it your purpose to eliminate your destructive self-beliefs. To create genuine healing you have to perceive that child you used to be with empathy and love.

Consider your feelings about your inner child, that little girl or boy that you used to be. Do you think about that child with love and compassion? Do you like that child, or do you look at that child with dislike or disgust? Do you avoid looking at pictures of yourself as a child?

In our first therapy session Ted referred to himself as a "high roller." He had made a great deal of money buying and selling companies. He wore the best clothes and drove the fastest cars. He was also quite proud of his many love exploits.

Despite his lifestyle and outward appearance, Ted was depressed. He appeared very self-confident on the outside, but his self-esteem was actually quite low. You see, Ted had an intense fear of Arthur.

Arthur was the name everyone used for Ted when he was a little boy. His parents called him Arthur as did his teachers and peers. Ted hated the little boy he used to be. He reported that he was overweight and nerdy as a child. He indicated that other boys picked on him because he was afraid to fight. He recalled an entire school year where he did without lunch because a bully took it and dared him to resist or tell anyone. As he shared the story, it became clear that the bully took much more than his lunch that year.

Ted also said his father disapproved of him as not being manly enough. The father was a furniture delivery man and would require Ted's help during the summer when school was out. When Ted would have trouble lifting his end of a piece of furniture, the father would ridicule him as being weak.

Since early adulthood, Ted had been running away from Arthur. He had created a lifestyle that was the total opposite of his childhood image. He felt disgust whenever he would think about Arthur. Whenever he said the name, he had a look of disdain on his face.

Unfortunately, Ted continued to carry Arthur with him wherever he went. Inside he still saw himself as that overweight, nerdy, weak kid, despite his elaborate, high-roller lifestyle. He consistently referred to his childhood self as Arthur and his adulthood self as Ted to further the distance between the two self-images.

I asked Ted to remember a time that was particularly hard for Arthur. He recalled a time when he was fourteen years old. He said that he had just moved to a new school and was trying to fit in. After a basketball game several "popular" boys were going to a local snack shop. He tagged along with them, thinking that he might finally fit in. He was the last one to get his order and the other boys had gone outside. When he went outside to join them, they were running off, laughing about the fact that they had ditched him. He said he felt a deep sense of shame as he walked home alone. As he told the story his face revealed that the memory still generated shame.

I knew that before he could improve his self-esteem, Ted would need to gain a better perspective of Arthur. Ted seemed to have a one dimensional, terribly negative view of himself as a child. He needed to develop compassion for that child, so I told him "The Parable of the Time Machine."

The Parable of the
Time Machine

❧ ❧

You had noticed the old Victorian house many, many times since it was on your route to work. It was surrounded by neatly trimmed bushes and a manicured lawn. The porch was particularly graceful with fancy posts and bright white trim that looked more like delicate lace than actual wood. As you drove past each morning, you tended to slow down just a bit and fantasized about the possible rooms inside with high ceilings, polished wood floors and Victorian furniture with doilies.

You also imagined the owner of such a home. No one was ever outside, so your mental images were all you had. You tended to picture a thin, graceful and proper elderly lady, one who matched the prim and proper look of the home.

You began to look at the house with new interest when you heard the rumors. First, you heard that the owner wasn't a prim little old lady at all, but was actually an eccentric, disheveled, middle-aged man. You heard he was single and somewhat of a recluse. A little later you heard he was an inventor, that strange noises could sometimes be heard from the basement, and that an occasional bright flash of light could be seen coming from the lower windows. Then you saw the dog.

That morning you were on your normal route to work and were passing by the house. As you glanced over, you saw a little dog in front of the porch. More accurately, this dog was hanging off the porch. It was on a leash, which had gotten wedged into one of the ornate curly wood panels. The dog's little back paws were on the ground, but it couldn't get its front paws down far enough to release the tension from its neck. This was a pretty little dog with fairly long straight hair, white with brown spots. Right now, the scene was not so pretty, as the little pup twisted against the leash. Strangulation would just be a matter of time.

The odd rumors about the house didn't enter your mind as you wheeled into the driveway. Turning off the engine, you jumped out of the car and ran over to the helpless pup. It didn't take much effort for you to free the leash and let the little dog breathe. As you held the leash, the front door opened.

He fit the rumors perfectly-a middle-aged man with odd-fitting, unkempt clothes and a head of hair reminiscent of Albert Einstein. He called for his dog before speaking to you and scooped him up into his arms. After making sure his little companion was okay, the man turned to you and thanked you profusely for your rescue. He introduced himself as Walter Sheffield. You noticed that he seemed nervous, probably because of the close call, but otherwise appeared genuinely nice. Mr. Sheffield then invited you inside, saying something about owing you a debt. You were actually considering accepting his invitation. After all, you had always wanted to see the inside of the house, and he did seem innocent enough. Then you remembered you were on your way to work and would already be a little late. When he asked if you would be willing to stop by on your way home from work for tea, your mouth spoke the words, "All right. About 5:30" before your brain fully engaged.

As your mind began to clear, all the reasons you shouldn't go back to this man's house became readily apparent. How could you have said yes? You could just drive past it and he would never know the difference. You did your good deed; now you didn't owe him anything. After all, he was a stranger and what about the odd rumors? But he did seem very nice and innocent in an odd sort of way.

You didn't actually decide to keep your promise until your car turned into the driveway. You could see that he was waiting on the porch with two cups and a tea pitcher on the table. The little dog was cradled in his arms. He waved when he saw you. Now you couldn't even back out of the drive without being obviously rude.

After brief re-introductions, you and Mr. Sheffield sat on the porch and carried on a pleasant-enough conversation. He let you know that he had moved here several years ago, adding that the peaceful, little town seemed to help him think more creatively. He said he was an inventor with several minor patents; and the royalties had allowed him to buy the house and fund his newest project. You listened more intently as you remembered the rumors of noises and flashes of light. Now he was getting to the interesting part-his newest invention. He nonchalantly announced that it was a time machine. That's right. He said his newest project was a time machine and that it worked quite well.

He spelled out in great detail the limits or boundaries under which he would allow such a machine to be used. He said that he would destroy the machine before he would allow anyone to use it to get rich. He also said he would be very afraid to let anyone use it to change major events of history because the implications would be unpredictable. That made sense. He seemed to have put a lot of thought into the possibility of great and horrible uses of such a machine. He then concluded his discourse by saying that he had decided that he would only allow this great machine to be used for "emotional healing."

"Emotional healing? What do you mean by that? "

His voice softened, and his gaze became more intent. "I've not always been a recluse" he noted as he raised one eyebrow. "I've known so many people in my time, myself included, that have carried great pain because of childhood wounds. Sometimes they have experienced abuse from those entrusted to love them, sometimes from neglect, criticism, or tragedy. There are so many ways that a little heart can be bruised; and once that bruise sets in, it can last a lifetime."

Your eyes had become fixed on an ant that was exploring a floor board. You were trying not to react to his words-words that spoke to your heart, to your wound. He continued that his machine would allow users to go back in time to a moment in their childhood when they had experienced the most hurt-a time when the child most needed the help, advice, support, or the love of a kind-hearted adult. Through the use of the time machine, the user could be that kind-hearted adult. The user would, of course, know the child and everything he or she had been going through. The child could not know that this supportive adult was actually the adult she would become. The user could spend time with the wounded child. She could use the benefit of her adult perspective, her life experience to help that child, to help heal that wounded heart.

Your words came automatically, "Can I use your machine? I need to heal some of my own wounds."

He replied softly, "I thought you might."

You sit quietly in the fully enclosed booth. He had explained that the process would take about thirty minutes to initiate. You would need to wait here until the time shift occurs. You have been given an identity, perhaps a friendly neighbor or a school teacher. You will be some person who would have an excuse to have contact with that little girl, your "cover" so to speak.

Applying the Parable

Now take thirty minutes to anticipate your time with that wounded young child that used to be you. You have thirty minutes to think about what you would want to say to him. How will you relate to him? What will you want to help him feel? Would you reassure him? Would you try to help him feel better about himself, to feel smarter, more capable? Would you want to help him feel important or loveable?

Think about it now. Close your eyes and imagine spending time with the child that used to be you. Try to picture yourself at that age where life was most difficult. If possible, get a photograph of yourself from about that time. Also, picture the house you lived in at that time. Remember what the rooms looked like and felt like. Take a moment to find a place where you won't be disturbed, and do this exercise now. Experience your encounter with the little boy that used to be you.

Now, imagine that you have that little boy living inside you today. Remember, all people, no matter how old, no matter what they do, have a little boy or a little girl living inside them. It's the part of us that is playful. It's also the part that is vulnerable to hurt.

What if you said the same things to yourself today that you would say to that child in the story? What if you gave yourself the same reassurances? What if you showed yourself the same compassion? What if you said those things to yourself that you would say to help the child's self-esteem?

Of course, it would take you time to begin believing those things. You would have to say those truths over-and-over to yourself. Going back to the time machine example, wouldn't you have to repeat those positive things to that little boy that used to be you as well? He wouldn't believe you at first either, but he would be worth persistent effort. So are you.

If that little child is living inside you, then what kind of things have you actually been saying to him? Aren't the statements you say in your thoughts actually like saying those things to the child? In a sense, you may have continued emotionally abusing that child by thinking harsh, self-critical statements. Do you think it might be time to stop the abuse? Can you stop it now?

When Ted imagined himself going back in time to encounter Arthur, he began by encouraging him to be stronger, as if trying to make him more masculine. As he continued the exercise, he began to look at Arthur, really look at him. Ted started to recognize that Arthur actually had many positive qualities. The realities of being bullied by other kids and, worse, by his own father, began to dawn on him. Ted began to see the young boy's pain.

His first reaction was an expression of grief for the boy and the shame he experienced; but soon, Ted expressed anger at the bullies and toward his father. Finally his attention shifted again to Arthur.

As Ted imagined what he would say to the little boy, his statements began to shift from corrective urging to accepting support. Ted gradually developed a kinder attitude toward the child he previously hated.

The shift in attitude was apparent during that session, but it wasn't complete. He still had struggles in the following weeks, but his compassion gradually grew. When I last saw Ted, he said his mood and attitude were much better. His drive to be a "high roller" had lessened considerably. I knew Ted had experienced healing when, as he said good-by, he smiled and commented, "You can call me Arthur, if you like."

Here is the homework that I gave to Ted. He wrote and then re-wrote his letter as his attitude changed toward Arthur. Put some thought into your letter. Lay it down for a few days and then re-read it. You may want to revise yours several times as well.

1. If you could go back in time, as in this exercise, what would you say to that child that you used to be? You know what he or she is going through. You know what he or she is feeling. What would you say? What would you want to help him or her feel? What messages would you want to convey to that child about who he or she is? Write the answers to these questions as a conversation to that child. You might want to write it as a letter.

----

2. Compare the messages you said above to the messages you say to yourself every day in your mind. First, write summary statements that would convey to that little boy or girl. Write them in "You are..." type sentences. Then, write the contrasting statements that you make to yourself in your mind now. Also, write these in "You are..." type sentences. For each statement in Part A, make a contrasting negative statement in Part B. Then examine the differences.

A. Statements you would make to the little boy or little girl that you used to be.

a. _____

b. _____

c. _____

d. _____

e. _____

f. _____

B. Negative statements you do make to yourself in your thoughts.

a. _____

b. _____

c. _____

d. _____

e. _____

f. _____

Monitor your thoughts during this week. Watch for any negative self-statements. If you catch yourself saying negative or self-critical messages to yourself, you need to think about the fact that you are actually saying those things to that little boy or girl. Without intending to do so, you are continuing to hurt that child inside you.

You can use the rubber band technique to help catch your negative self-statements. Remember that you are wearing the rubber band for that little girl or little boy!

When you experience compassion for that little child you used to be, you will be appropriately motivated to work on this healing process. You will feel a sense of purpose in this work. That child would be worth it. You are worth it.

Concluding Comments:

Any reader of self-help books is familiar with the concept of the "inner child." We are familiar with that child-like part of us that is playful or vulnerable. We often forget that everyone else also has an inner child who reacts similarly to our own. A wound of the heart often causes us to keep the child in the shadows, however. We don't want to look at the child because we don't like the child. We see the child as defective, dirty, or unlovable because, without conscious intention, we placed all our negative self-beliefs on that child.

My clients often find this homework assignment to be difficult at first. Their first attempts at a letter may sound corrective or encouraging but not compassionate, loving or nurturing. As they continue the process (sometimes re-writing the letter several times), they begin to develop that compassion. They begin to see things they like about the child. You will know you are finished with this week's assignment when you genuinely feel compassion or love for your inner child. Write, re-write, leave it, and then go back to it until you experience those feelings.

The eccentric inventor has shared several truths. These include:

1. The child was innocent and undeserving of the negative treatment.

2. The child was hurt.
3. The child was helpless.
4. The child needed someone to help him or her to heal those wounds.
5. You could be that someone for the child.
6. You can be that someone now.
7. To do that, you have to feel compassion for that child, the child that is within you.

Chapter 6
Understanding Your True Worth

You made all the delicate, inner parts of my body and knit me together in my mother's womb.
Psalm 139:13

Many people question, "Am I worthwhile, or am I worthless? Do I have the same worth as other human beings?" These are questions whose answers are first formulated during childhood. The child's answers come from parents, grandparents, caretakers, teachers and other children.

The first answers come from parents. A parent's words and behaviors place a price tag on the child. This child is wanted, loved, and precious. That child is in the way, not wanted, or criticized. It is as if the parents or caretakers place a price tag on the child's neck.

The child automatically accepts the price tag placed upon her as her true worth. How would she know any different? The child then keeps that price tag on her neck throughout life, unless something or someone intervenes. That price tag changes everything.

You have a price tag as well. It was your value, as indicated by the behavior of your parents and others. Their behaviors told you whether you were worthwhile or worthless. It wasn't a true message of your worth, but it felt that way to you.

To heal your heart wound, you have to recognize that those messages of your worth were actually a reflection of the problems of those around you. You have to establish your own internal definition of your worth.

Mary Anne did not want to be in my office. Her primary physician had prescribed antidepressants but said he would not give her another prescription unless she came in to see me. She didn't trust easily, and I would later understand why.

She had never met her biological father. One day without warning, her mother dropped her and her younger sister at the mailbox of her grandmother's house and drove off. They watched their mother drive into the distance and then walked down the long driveway to their new home. The grandmother, whom they had rarely seen, had no idea they were coming. Mary Anne didn't see her mother until several years later. The grandmother took care of the children's physical needs out of obligation, but frequently she complained that the two girls had intruded on her life.

I could easily understand why Mary Anne would feel unwanted, unlovable, and worthless. She frequently asked me to help her understand what was wrong with her that made others reject her. Mary Anne wanted to know how to fix herself so that others would love her. Sadly, she couldn't remember anyone who really acted as if she had value.

Before her twentieth birthday, Mary Anne would be sexually abused by three different men, one of whom was a pastor she had approached for counseling. She then married a man who was extremely emotionally and physically abusive. I remember that she arrived for several sessions wearing sunglasses because her husband had given her black eyes. Mary Anne reported that her husband's favorite phrase was that she was "a worthless piece of s**t."

Despite the fact that one of her abusers was a pastor, Mary Anne had always been involved in church and believed in God. One day she told me that she prayed every day that God would love her. I told her that I believed she was praying for the wrong thing, and suggested that she pray that God would help her realize how much He already loved her. She hesitantly agreed to try.

I wanted to help Mary Anne separate her actual worth from the messages she had received from her parents and others. I wanted to help her recognize that she was worthwhile, even though so many had treated her as worthless. I told her "The Parable of The Violin That No One Wanted."

The Parable of the
Violin No One Wanted

&~&

Once there was a family that bought an old house. The prior owners had moved out of the house some time earlier, so this new family never met them. On the day they moved in, they had some items that they wanted to store in the attic. When they climbed up the attic stairs, they found that the previous owners had left some junk piled in one corner. The new owners didn't have time to go through the stuff and throw it away, so they just stacked their things around the leftover pile. They didn't think of it again.

After several years, the family decided to do some spring cleaning. They planned to have a yard sale to get rid of some of the things they had stored in the attic. When they went up to get their items, they saw the pile of things left by the previous owners. They decided they might as well try to sell those things too. Perhaps they could make a little extra money.

As they sorted out the pile, they found several items they could sell including an old violin in a case. The violin looked in pretty good shape, but the case was very dusty and all scratched up. They decided to put a $20.00 price tag on it and see what they could get.

On the day of the yard sale they put all the items on tables, and people began to stop and browse. They sold many of their items and were about to call it a day. There were a few stragglers milling around the tables checking for any last minute buys. A car pulled over and a tall, thin older man got out. He too browsed the tables for a while.

He came to the table with the violin in the opened case. It seems no one had needed a fiddle this morning, not even for $20.00. He leaned over and studied the dusty violin for a couple of minutes before he spoke to the owner behind the table. He inquired, "Do you mind if I take it out of the case?"

"No," the owner replied, "Help yourself."

He picked the violin up very slowly and carefully, as if it were going to fall apart in his hands.

"May I tune it?" the old man asked.

"If you can," the owner answered.

The old man slowly tuned the violin until he seemed to be satisfied with each string. The owner waited patiently since most of the crowd had dispersed; and this seemed like the most promising chance of getting rid of the instrument.

"May I play it?" the old man asked.

"Sure, see how it sounds," was the owner's reply, now feeling that a sale was in the making.

The old man slowly placed the violin under his chin and began to play. The straggling shoppers stopped and stared as the notes drifted across the yard in the spring sunshine. The old man crafted the most beautiful music for several minutes before he stopped. He lowered the violin from his chin and placed it very gently back in its case. The owner moved in to make the sale. "You make that thing sing, mister" he said with a grin. "You can have it for only $20.00."

The older man's face was somber. "I can't give you $20.00 for that violin," he replied.

"Well, how about $15.00?" said the owner, now thinking a sale was slipping away.

"Sir, you don't understand." noted the old man, still serious. "I can't take that violin from you for $20.00. It wouldn't be right." Looking directly into the owner's eyes, he lowered his voice and smiled slightly, "I don't know how you came upon that violin, but you don't know what you have there. You see, that violin is a Stradivarius. You can tell from the markings in the sound hole. It was made by Antonio Stradivari in Cremona. His instruments are the best in the world. You see, his mark is there in the sound hole. This violin is worth at least $1,000,000 and probably much more. It's a very, very special instrument and very precious. You just didn't realize what you had."

Applying the Parable

The violin had always been precious. It was valuable because of its creator. The violin was valuable because its creator only made precious instruments, and it carried the unmistakable mark of that creator. The earlier homeowners who left it in the attic obviously didn't know what they had and treated it like trash. The new owners didn't know what they had either and left it in the attic with the trash. The yard sale shoppers who left it on the table didn't know what they were leaving behind. They treated it as if it was not even worth $20.00. It took the old man to recognize the violin's value. He didn't have to play it to recognize that it was precious. The old man knew it was precious because he knew about its creator. He knew that it had the mark of its creator.

You may be like the violin. You may have grown up in a family that wasn't able to recognize your true value. They may have acted as if you were in the way or just something to be tolerated. Or they may have made you feel that you couldn't do anything right or were always messing up. Later in life, you may have dealt with others who also acted as you weren't worth much, who acted as if you were trash.

It's important to remember that the violin never actually lost its value. It was just as valuable when it was left in a corner of the attic as it would have been in a symphony hall. It was still valuable when it was passed over by the rest of the customers in the yard sale. The creator had left his mark on it, and that made all the difference.

Every child is valuable. Each child is as valuable as any other child. We all know this to be true. There is no defect, deformity, characteristic, or behavior that can make a child less valuable. We also know this to be true. A child's actual value is not diminished when her family doesn't recognize or act as if she is valuable. You know this to be true.

The child is hurt, of course. The child learns to believe that she is not valuable. Such lessons are learned deeply. Such beliefs are hard to change. Just because a belief is deeply learned doesn't mean that it is true.

Think back to your childhood experiences. Imagine the possibility that you may have learned inaccurate beliefs about your value because of those experiences. Just let yourself entertain the possibility that the messages you received about yourself were lies told by people whose perceptions and behaviors were possibly warped by their own childhood wounds. Consider the fact that the way one is treated does not define that person's value.

You can recognize that this is true when you think about all the many children who are abused every day. You know that those children don't deserve to be abused or mistreated. They are valuable. They are precious, despite the fact that they are treated badly. Consider the fact that this truth also applies to you. It does apply to you. It always has.

Of course, the creator of the violin is a metaphor for our Creator. There is an old saying that says "God doesn't make junk." I think we might even go further and say that God's creations are always precious. As humans, we do have many faults; and none of us are perfect. But we do have the mark of our Creator. You have that mark.

So did Mary Anne. It took a lot of work for her to realize this, and the process was gradual. Eventually, however, she was able to recognize her value and to treat herself in accordance with that value. The change wasn't miraculous, but I could see it. She simply treated herself with the same kindness that she had previously offered to others. Come to think of it, I guess that was miraculous.

The following homework is designed to help you examine and challenge any negative beliefs you have about your worth or value.

REGARDING THE VIOLIN

1. Consider the following statements made about the violin by the homeowners and the shoppers. Then consider the truth about the violin's value.

They Said:	The Truth Was:
It is worthless.	It was precious.
It's a waste of space.	It was important.
It's old and dirty.	It deserved great care.
It's in the way.	It is valuable.

REGARDING YOU

2. Now think about any negative messages you have received about your value. These messages could have come from child-

hood or adult experiences. Then generate truth statements about your worth or value from your Creator's perspective. To help you with this, I have listed some scripture passages that tell you what your Creator thinks of you.

For God so loved the world that He gave his only begotten Son, that whosoever believes in him should not perish, but have eternal life. John 3:16

How precious are your thoughts about me, O God...Psalm 139:17

Nothing can ever separate us from His love. Romans 8:35-39

Come to me, all of you who are weary and carry heavy burdens, and I will give you rest.
Matthew 11:28

For I am convinced that neither death nor life, neither angels nor demons, neither the present nor the future, nor any powers, neither height nor depth, nor anything else in all creation, will be able to separate us from the love of God that is in Christ Jesus our Lord. Romans 8:38

(The Lie) Those from your past said:	(The Truth) What your creator thinks about You:
_____	_____
_____	_____
_____	_____
_____	_____
_____	_____
_____	_____

3. Copy the Truth statements on small cards that you can keep in your pocket or pocketbook. Each day, read the Truth

statements to yourself several times. Let your Creator speak to you this week through the exercise. You might also try praying this week that God will help you realize the extent of His love for you, that He will help you feel that love radiating through you.

Concluding Comments:

The spiritual or religious foundation of this story is obvious. Most of my clients relate very well to that world view. You may have different beliefs, and that's fine. Even if you don't share a "creator" belief system, you can benefit from the story, if you believe in the inherent worth of a human being. If you believe that human beings have inherent value and you recognize that some families treat their children as if they have no value, you will connect to the story. You will see that your treatment had nothing to do with your actual worth.

The violin shared several important truths. These are as follows:

1. Sometimes people fail to recognize the true worth of an object or a person.
2. Sometimes precious things and people are treated as worthless.
3. That negative treatment doesn't alter the person's actual worth.
4. You were made by your creator, just exactly as every other human being on earth.
5. Your creator only makes precious instruments.
6. You are as precious as any other human being.
7. You have, and have always had, the mark of your creator. It is unmistakable.
8. There have probably been some people in your life who have had the wisdom to recognize that mark and your inherent value. Their behaviors con-

veyed the message that you were precious. Listen to them.

A Summary of Part 1:

In the previous chapters, a little girl, two evil psychologists, a violin and an eccentric inventor have revealed the following:

1. Your negative beliefs about yourself were learned from your childhood experiences.
2. Those experiences actually reflected the problems of those around you, not problems with you.
3. Your negative self-beliefs have created enormous pain in your life and will continue to create such pain unless corrected.
4. Your negative childhood experiences would have had the same impact on any other child.
5. Your actual value is established by the fact that your creator only creates precious instruments.
6. Everything is impacted by your self-beliefs.
7. You must make it your purpose, your mission, your priority to attack those negative self-beliefs and replace them with more healthy, positive self-beliefs. You must replace the lies with the truth!
8. When you replace your negative self-beliefs with the truth, you heal your wound of the heart. Since this change is difficult, you have to want it..... a lot!
9. The rest of your life depends on it!

"The Parable of the Violin Nobody Wanted" was inspired by the poem, "The Touch of the Master's Hand" by Myra "Brooks" Welch (1921).

Part 2
Perception

I hope that you now understand the origin of your negative self-esteem and the devastating power of your negative self-beliefs. I also hope that you have begun to look at the child you used to be with greater understanding and compassion. If so, you should be significantly motivated to rid yourself of your negative beliefs and to establish a more healthy and positive self-esteem. This should now be your purpose.

In Part 2, we will address the role of perception in healing your wounds of the heart. We will be working on helping you perceive yourself differently. We will also be working on helping you to perceive your day-to-day experiences differently.

Everything you experience in this life is determined by perception. Perception is your brain's attempt to make sense out of the stimuli that are hitting your five senses of vision, hearing, taste, smell, and touch. Your senses pick up stimuli and send them to your brains as electrical signals. Your brain then takes those signals and processes them to allow you to make sense out of them.

The process of perception doesn't end with the identification of physical objects. We also utilize perception when we are trying to interpret the meaning of an event. Our brains compare each new event to similar experiences from our past. For example, your husband's anger may trigger feelings of panic if you were physically abused as a child whenever your father became angry.

Sometimes, however, our brains misinterpret the signals coming into our senses. A wound of the heart often creates perceptual misperceptions which then worsen the wound.   In Part 2 you will be asked to consider some everyday examples of perceptual distortions. You will also be introduced to a struggling baseball player, a prejudiced judge, and a strange but wise old man who will help you examine your perceptions and see yourself and your world differently.

Chapter 7
Seeing More Than You Actually See

People only see what they are prepared to see.
Ralph Waldo Emerson

Lasting change only occurs when perception changes. When a couple or family seeks marriage or family counseling, they do so because they feel their relationships are in trouble and they want them to improve. In counseling they determine the nature of the problem and the changes needed to correct that problem. The first changes occur when they recognize that they need to behave differently, and they make an effort to do so. They may try harder to listen to each other, or they may try to be more affectionate or kind. When they do this, the relationships often improve. There may be fewer conflicts or they may feel closer. They think that things are better. This conscious effort to change and the subsequent improvement in behavior is called a first order change.

A first order change is necessary but never sufficient. It is not sufficient because it is always temporary. The family will act better as long as they consciously think about doing so. Unfortunately, after a while the demands and stresses of life distract them from their efforts; and their behaviors revert back to the old patterns. They feel that they are "back to square one." In fact, they are.

The marriage and family counselor strives for a second order change. A second order change occurs when the family members gain a new and different perception of each other. They actually see some aspect of the other person that they didn't see before. They perceive each other differently. This new perception is relatively permanent. Once you see something, you cannot go back to not seeing it.

Once you know something in a new way, you are changed. You can't go back to not knowing it.

The distinction of first order and second order change also applies to the process of healing your wounds of the heart. A low self-esteem may be elevated temporarily by positive self-talk, repeating positive affirmations, or even a successful life-event. The boost feels good for a short time, but the self-esteem soon drops to its original level. The change is good but temporary.

Permanent healing of a wound of the heart requires a second order change, thus a change in perception. To achieve true healing, you must perceive yourself differently. Once you know yourself in a new way, you are changed. You can't go back to your old destructive perceptions.

The first step in changing a perception is the recognition that the perception may be inaccurate. This is difficult because the perception feels so real. We feel quite certain that we are seeing the situation accurately. If our perceptions are challenged, we argue that we just know the truth. We unconsciously work to maintain our existing perceptions even when we have no factual evidence to support those them.

I had a client, Michelle, who had been coming in for counseling for several months. She was a pleasant, likable woman of about 40. Michelle came in because of her discomfort in social situations. She felt socially uncomfortable because she believed that others judged her or that they looked at her in a disapproving way.

Michelle avoided social situations whenever she could. There was no one that she would truly consider a friend. She did some things with a cousin, but not often. Michelle sometimes said that she preferred her own company over that of most people she knew, but occasionally she admitted that she was actually very lonely.

Michelle complained that social activities were just too difficult, feeling that she was on stage all the time. It seemed that the loneliness was easier to bear than the judgment of the world.

I asked Michelle about specific situations where she believed others had disapproved of her or judged her. She indicated that her mother had been very hard to please, but that she felt much closer to her father who was a pastor of a small church. Michelle indicated that both parents frequently pointed out that the church members watched the pastor's family and that misbehavior on her part could cost her father his job. The phrase, "What would people think?" was used liberally by her mother. Michelle said she felt as if she lived in a fishbowl through most of her childhood.

Michelle then told me that she found out at age ten that she was adopted. She said that her mother blurted it out during an argument. The argument was actually between her parents; but Michelle tried to intervene to defend her father, and her mother turned on her. She said that she often felt that her mother was too critical of her father, but that she was only critical when no one was around to hear it. In front of others she was always kind and gentle.

I asked Michelle about events in her adult life that suggested that others were judging her. She related several events. In each one, her "evidence" of other's disapproval consisted of a certain facial expression or a vague comment. She would then interpret the evidence to mean that the person was feeling negatively about her.

I tried to help Michelle realize that she was "mind reading." As we discussed in Chapter 1, the term mind reading refers to the times when we assume what someone is thinking or feeling when we actually don't know. Of course, we can't actually read someone's mind; but we assume their thoughts or feelings, based on facial expressions, vague statements, or tone of voice.

Michelle argued that her assumptions were on target and that she could "just tell what they were thinking." She stood steadfast in her beliefs. In order to illustrate the process of perceptual misinterpretation, I shared some personal experiences.

The Parable of
The Object on the Road

ॐॐ

One afternoon my wife and I were driving in the country on a long straight road. It was late in the day, almost dusk; but I could still see without my headlights.

Far ahead, I saw a brown, crumpled object lying in the grass on the side of the road. I didn't give it much thought as I was involved in a conversation with my wife. As my car approached the object, I could see it a bit more clearly; and I made it out to be a dead animal on the side of the road. I could barely make out the head, body and possibly legs of the poor creature. When I got closer to the object, I was able to see it clearly; and I saw that it was actually a crumpled cardboard box lying in the grass.

Like most drivers, I had had such experiences many times before. This time, however, I saw a deeper meaning. This time, I asked myself "why?" Why did I see a crumpled cardboard box as a dead animal? What actually happened?

When I first saw the object, my brain began the process of perception. My brain was trying to make sense of the object, even though I wasn't even consciously thinking about it. I was still consciously focused on my conversation.

As the visual stimulus gained more definition of shape and shadow, my brain identified the object as a dead animal. My brain actually filled in the blanks to see a head, body and legs on a cardboard box.

Why did I see the object as a dead animal? I saw it as such because I had seen dead animals on the road before. The object was brown, crumpled, and lying in the grass. In the past, such objects have actually been unfortunate animals that have been hit by cars. My brain filled in the blanks to see what it expected to see from past experience.

Consider what would have happened if I had been traveling on a road that led to a cardboard recycling factory. Imagine that I knew that boxes sometimes blew off trucks hauling them to the factory. Under those circumstances, I might have seen the object as a cardboard box, even if it was actually a dead animal.

In the process of perception, our brains work hard to establish meaning for the stimuli coming into our senses. Sometimes, in this effort, the brain will go so far as to fill in the blanks, thus 'seeing' something that isn't really there. But it will always fill in the missing information in accordance with our prior experiences. Our prior experiences create our current expectations, which alter our perceptions of events.

Now let's apply this to you. Did your childhood experiences include people who were critical, judgmental or rejecting? If so, you may have an expectation that the people you encounter today will treat you the same way. Do you tend to believe that others are thinking critical or judgmental things about you, or that they don't want to be with you or don't like you? You can observe other's behaviors, but you can't actually know their thoughts or feelings. Unless they have actually verbalized such negative things, you have missing information. You view the person's behaviors, your brain fills in the blanks and you then see the person criticizing you or rejecting you. You assume that you can tell what the person is thinking about you when, in fact, you can't. This is mind reading. No one is immune to mind reading.

Applying the Parable

Consider the possibility that many of your negative life events were hurtful because you misperceived them. What if (at least sometimes) you perceived someone as being critical, disapproving or uncaring when they were actually not having those feelings at all? What if you filled in the blanks to see rejection, criticism, or disapproval; and you were wrong? How many times have you felt hurt in social interactions because of your misperceptions?

Michelle recognized intellectually that she made assumptions about other's thoughts or feelings about her but maintained that she was right most of the time. I challenged her to examine the times where she felt someone was disapproving of her. Michelle was to ask herself what evidence she actually had about their disapproving thoughts or feelings and then to ask herself if that evidence would stand up in a court of law. In other words, was it clear and unmistakable? If she actually did not have facts to back up her perceptions, she was mind reading.

As we worked together, Michelle became more adept at catching herself when she made mind reading assumptions. She saw that her assumptions always made her think that others were being critical or disapproving of her, which was what she expected. With some coaching, Michelle understood that those expectations were based on her childhood experiences of her mother's criticism and the many messages from her parents that she was being watched by the people of the church.

Over time, Michelle's expectations of disapproval changed. She became much less likely to perceive judgment from others and became more comfortable in social situations.

Despite her new perceptions, Michelle still associated social situations with anxiety. Another step in the treatment process was necessary. Michelle needed to face her fears by putting herself in more social situations. With my urging, she did force herself to engage in social activity with gradually increasing frequency. Each time she engaged in a social event, where nothing catastrophic happened, Michelle experienced a greater sense of comfort. By facing her fearful situation (social interactions) she was able to conquer her anxiety. Michelle couldn't have done that, however, if she hadn't learned to question her perceptions that others were judging her.

You may feel as if you *know* how other people feel about you. You may be right, but you may be wrong. Consider how many times you have filled in the blanks in your social interactions and incorrectly assumed that you were being criticized or rejected. How many times have you been hurt by inaccurate mind reading or have lost potentially good relationships because of mind reading?

From this point forward, I want you to try to question your assumptions about what other people are thinking. This will not be easy, but you can learn the habit by practicing such questioning on a daily basis. Sometimes you will catch your assumptions and sometimes you won't; but by limiting your assumptions, you will be able to be more objective about other's reactions. You will gradually begin to see evidence that your assumptions have been inaccurate, and over time you will find yourself becoming more comfortable in social situations.

Another area where we make assumptions is when considering the future. We tend to make assumptions about what is going to happen in the future. Predictions of the future are also assumptions because we cannot, of course, actually predict future events. Assumptions of the future are also shaped by our expectations and our beliefs. If we have experienced a history of negative events, we assume that the future will hold negative events. If we hold the belief that "nothing good ever happens to me," we assume that the future holds only bad outcomes. Since we can't actually predict the future, the only accurate answer to a question about future events is, "I don't know."

The following homework exercises are designed to help you establish the habit of questioning your assumptions and, thus, to stop filling in the blanks.

1. This week watch for possible perceptual distortions. Watch to see how many times you make assumptions in your life. Notice those times when you have only part of the facts of a situation but act as if you have all the facts. If you conclude that someone is thinking something or feeling something and that person has not actually told you what they are thinking or feeling, you are assuming. If you believe something is going to happen, but you cannot actually predict the future, you are assuming. Remember that you always fill in the blanks to create a perception that fits with your prior experiences and expectations.

    To avoid assumptions, you need to try to limit yourself to the facts that you, or anyone else could observe. One way to catch an assumption is to ask yourself if you would have the facts to prove your conclusion in a court of law "beyond a reasonable doubt." Anything less constitutes an assumption.

2. List some assumptions you have made recently or in the distant past. Particularly note examples where you have done mind reading- that is assuming what people are thinking when you cannot actually read their minds. Remember, the only mind you can actually read is your own.

    EXAMPLES OF MY MIND READING ASSUMPTIONS:
    (Ex: Sarah doesn't like me, because she didn't speak to me.)

    _____
    _____
    _____
    _____
    _____
    _____
    _____
    _____
    _____

3. Review the above assumptions. Go back to the exercises at the end of the story of "The Stupid Little Girl." Look at your belief statements in Part B, on page 40. Do the assumption statements you wrote above seem to reflect the beliefs you recorded in Part B? Notice that your assumptions serve to strengthen those beliefs you recorded in Part B. The Mind Reading served as a Belief Keeper for those beliefs. Remember that those beliefs were learned and predominantly inaccurate.

4. Consider the mind reading assumptions you wrote in number 2, again. Think about what you actually observed and what you assumed or "filled in the blanks." Try to consider other possible explanations for the other person's behaviors. What might they have actually been thinking or feeling underneath those behaviors? Try to come up with three examples.

a. What I believed the people were thinking or feeling:

1. _____
2. _____
3. _____

b. What I actually observed with my senses (the actual facts) in each situation:

1. _____
2. _____
3. _____

c. Alternate possible explanations for each person's behaviors:

1. _____
2. _____
3. _____

5. List assumptions you have made where you were predicting the future. Any time you believed you knew what would happen in the future, you were assuming. Note assumptions you have made about the future:

_____
_____
_____
_____
_____
_____
_____
_____
_____
_____
_____

6. Think about your expectations for your life. With some thought, you will be able to identify patterns. Do you tend to expect good or bad things to happen? Do you tend to expect yourself to succeed or to fail? Do you expect others to like you and accept you, or to dislike you and not

accept you? Do you expect others to care about you and
your feelings, or to not care about you or your feelings?

7. Do you tend to get what you expect? Is it possible that
you fill in the blanks so that you see what you expect to
see? Is it possible that you pay more attention to those
times when your expectations are fulfilled and less atten-
tion to the events that don't coincide with your expecta-
tions?

Concluding Comments:

Most of my clients have difficulty questioning their assump-
tions. Like you and me, they have spent a lifetime making assump-
tions and believing them. It's all they've ever known.

Thinking about the fact that you have misperceived many
events can generate a bit of discomfort. You may not have been happy
or enjoyed your life. You may have even mentally abused yourself; but
at least you were familiar with this. There is a certain comfort in the
familiar, even when it is painful.

The homework exercises in this chapter are designed to help
you get started, but they can only take you so far. Nothing will take
the place of your day-to-day experience of noticing your assumptions,
making the connection between them and your core negative beliefs,
and reminding yourself that you actually don't know the truth. Be-
fore you can see the true reality, you have to be willing to question
the validity of your existing reality. That's tough. Try it anyway.

In the structured journal, you are asked to note some of the
day's events, your reactions to those events and an alternative truth.
Note any assumptions about other's thoughts or feelings and exam-
ine them in the journal.

Also, use the Rubber Band Technique this week whenever you
catch yourself making assumptions about what others are thinking.
(See page 225 for a complete explanation of this technique.) Each time
you pop the rubber band, remind yourself that you can't read minds
or predict the future.

The object by the side of the road conveyed several truths.
These are as follows:

1. The human brain is constantly engaged in the process of perception.

2. Perception is the brain's attempt to make sense out of the data collected by the five senses.

3. In the process of perception, the brain often takes the actual information collected by the senses and adds information not actually sensed to create meaning in the experience.

4. The added (not sensed) information always fits with the brain's assumptions or prior experiences.

5. The added information is often not accurate.

6. Since we don't realize that the information is inaccurate, we respond as if the information was factual or accurate.

7. Our prior experience with criticism or rejection causes our mind to add information to later events, which leads us to believe that we are being criticized or rejected.

Chapter 8
The Perception Deception

It's not what you look at that matters, it's what you see.
Henry David Thoreau

As you saw in Chapter 7, when given incomplete information, our brains fill in the blanks with information that is in agreement with our prior expectations. We often make inaccurate assumptions that others are being critical, judgmental, disapproving or rejecting. Those assumptions create unnecessary emotional pain and serve to maintain our wounds of the heart.

In this chapter you will learn that your wounds of the heart created even deeper distortions in your perception. You will see that heart wounds make some events look larger or more important, while making other events look smaller and less important. Such wounds also make certain events stand out in your mind, while causing other events to disappear from your awareness altogether.

Imagine that you have a lens through which you see the world. Everything you perceive is seen through that lens. When you see your life events you see them through your lens. You see your past, your present circumstances, and your future through that same lens. You see yourself through the lens as well. Everyone has such a lens.

If the lens were clear and accurate this would not be a problem. Unfortunately, your wound of the heart has distorted your lens. The negative events that wounded your self-esteem also distorted your lens, thus distorting your perception of reality. Being unaware of the lens distortion, you assumed you were seeing everything accurately. You reacted to what you saw. You couldn't know any better.

If you experienced messages that you were incompetent, your lens distortion makes your mistakes appear more negative or more important than they actually are. You also perceive your successes as less important or even as being pure luck or a fluke.

If you were rejected or neglected during childhood you may magnify the occasions where others are distant and minimize or ignore the times where others seem to like you or have a high regard for you.

In each instance your lens distortion magnifies some events while minimizing others. Your brain pays attention to those events that support its prior beliefs while ignoring or dismissing contradictory events. Remember that the human brain is a belief-maintaining mechanism. The distortion always serves to maintain your pre-existing beliefs. This is an example of the Belief Keeper of Selective Attention discussed in Chapter One.

A lens distortion can also produce a misinterpretation of events. You may perceive a particular event to mean that you are inadequate or unimportant and yet interpret the same event completely differently should it happen to someone else. For example, a mistake made by you may be perceived as evidence of your stupidity, while the same mistake made by someone else is perceived as a simple accident. The lens distortion alters the meaning you attach to the event. This perceptional distortion will be covered more in Chapter 10.

Another perceptual distortion occurs when you blame yourself for anything bad that happens. This is an example of the Belief Keeper of Blame Magnet. You become a blame magnet when you inaccurately perceive problems in life as your fault. If anything goes wrong your brain will find some way to place the blame on you.

The Blame Magnet tendency can be amazingly strong. During therapy, I have often observed normally logical clients blame themselves for events in a way that defies all logic, yet the client fails to see any problem with his interpretation. His words seem totally reasonable to him.

When I point out problems with the logic of Blame Magnet, the patient may intellectually agree, but maintain that it still feels like the event is his fault. His tendency to listen to his feelings, even when those feelings are not logical, is an example of the Belief Keeper of Emotional Compass (Discussed in Chapter 1).

If you experienced rejection or isolation during childhood, your lens will become distorted in a way that makes any relationship difficulties seem like evidence that you are difficult to love or unlikable. Again, you become a Blame Magnet, but here the blame focuses on your relationships. When people treat you badly, you feel certain that they did so because of a defect in you.

This self-blame tendency will defy all logic. For example, a woman is married to an alcoholic man. He was married twice before and had affairs while married to both of his previous wives. This woman and her husband have two children, but he has never shown them much attention, treating them as if they were an inconvenience. He then has an affair, leaves with the mistress, and stops any contact with the wife and their children. The woman concludes that his affair and his leaving were because she wasn't lovable enough. She doesn't take into account that he has done this in all his relationships or that he left their two children as well. She knows without doubt that their children are loveable. The woman attributes her husband's behavior toward the children as his fault, not the children's. Yet she feels deeply that his rejection of her was proof of her being unlovable. The woman's self-esteem wound is, thus, deepened.

To heal your wound of the heart, you must recognize that the wound created a distortion in your lens. You must learn to question your perceptions, particularly those that seem to reflect your wound. To heal you have to become aware of your particular lens distortions and the effects of those distortions. You can then begin to realize the types of misperceptions that are most likely to occur.

When we are aware of our particular lens distortions, we question ourselves when we see such events. Questions, such as the following, can help you identify and correct misperceptions created by a lens distortion. I have grouped the questions as they would apply to each particular Belief Keeper.

Selective Attention:
1. Am I focusing my attention on my mistakes or faults, while ignoring my successes or strengths?
2. What are my positive traits, efforts or behaviors?

3. Am I focusing on the negative statements made about me or my behaviors, while ignoring the positive feedback I have received?
4. Was my mistake as big a deal as I'm making it?

Emotional Compass:
1. Am I listening to my feelings or emotions about this situation, despite contradictory evidence or facts?
2. What do the facts tell me?
3. Are my feelings about this logical and would I feel the same way about someone else who was in my shoes?

Blame Magnet:
1. Am I ignoring other possible contributions to this negative event, while focusing only on my mistakes or contributions?
2. If the same thing happened to a good friend, would I think that it was her fault?
3. Is it really logical for me to place all the blame on myself for this negative circumstance?

There is an old saying that goes, "When your children are young they'll step on your toes, but when they get older, they'll step on your heart." I had a client named Paul who knew this idea well.

Paul's own father didn't provide much of an example for him. He and Paul's mother divorced when Paul was age three. He did pay child support and visited Paul and his sister occasionally for about four years after the divorce but rarely made contact after that point.

Paul said he always felt that he was a disappointment to his father. He said his father had a bad temper and criticized him frequently. He said he actually learned to dread the father's visits and felt some relief when they stopped. He felt guilty about those feelings.

He said he had always sworn to himself that he would be a better father than his dad was, and he tried to live up to his promise. Unfortunately, when he came in for our first appointment, he felt he had failed miserably.

Paul and his wife, Julie, had three children-one daughter and two sons. His daughter, the eldest, had never given them any trouble. She made good grades in school and seemed to be the model child. After college, she became a pharmacist, married, and was doing well.

His middle child had also done well. He graduated college and went into sales. He seemed to be successful and happy. He had recently become engaged to a girl that Paul and his wife really liked.

Paul's concern was with his youngest son, Jason. He was twenty-two when Paul came to see me. He had graduated from high school but barely made it. His list of troubles was long.

Jason began associating with a bad crowd when he was about thirteen years of age. He started smoking marijuana about that time. Later he moved up to pills, cocaine and, finally, meth. To fund his habits Jason broke into houses and cars, stealing anything he found. He was arrested twice as a juvenile but received light sentences or probation. At the time Paul came in to see me, Jason was serving a six month sentence for possession with intent to sell.

When he was eighteen Jason moved in with some friends. He rarely visited his parents and repelled any efforts they had made to help him. They had made many such efforts. They took him to several counselors and made two attempts at residential substance abuse treatment. Nothing worked. Paul and his wife worried and prayed.

The heartache of a troubled child is difficult enough, but the pain of self-blame is almost unbearable. Unfortunately, Paul believed that he carried all the blame for Jason's troubles squarely on his shoulders.

Paul scrutinized everything he had done since Jason was born. As he did so, he found many personal choices and behaviors that he could fault. He said he had worked too many hours and not been there enough in the early years. Paul sometimes felt that he had been too harsh, but sometimes felt he was too lenient. He blamed himself because his job required them to relocate when Jason was twelve. I listened as this man anguished that he should have seen Jason's problems earlier and that treatment might have been more effective at that point. Paul's words were like a whip which he used without mercy and his lashes were too many to count.

I tried to point out that there were several holes in Paul's logic. I first addressed his Belief Keeper of Blame Magnet. I noted that he placed no blame on Julie's parenting, even though she was as much a part of the parenting process as he was. He seemed to forget that he had also parented two other children who turned out quite well. Paul ignored all the influences in Jason's life other than his parenting, while focusing all his attention on his possible contributions. Finally, he knew other families with a troubled child but never assumed the problem stemmed from those parents being inadequate.

I noted that Paul's thinking also demonstrated the Belief Keeper of Selective Attention. As he recalled his interactions with Jason, those instances when his son was critical of his father stood out in vivid detail, while all the times when Paul loved and supported of his son faded from awareness. Paul's attention focused on his parenting mistakes, while his many efforts and the many nights he worried and prayed for Jason disappeared. When pressed, Paul admitted that he had made many efforts to help his son, but he immediately dismissed those efforts as ineffective.

Paul recognized the logic of my arguments, but didn't agree with my conclusion. He asserted that he just felt that he was the source of Jason's problems. He said that he just knew it in his gut. I tried to help Paul understand that this dependence on his feelings or emotions for truth was an example of Belief Keeper of Emotional Compass, and that it would always point in the direction of his prior negative self-beliefs.

Paul's perception of the situation was definitely distorted, and each distortion seemed to trace back to his own father's message that he was inadequate. Paul's lens distortion made him magnify any mistakes he may have made in parenting. It made him minimize his many efforts to be a good parent. The distortion made him magnify his responsibility in the creation of Jason's problems and minimize his wife's contributions. The distortion caused him to examine himself relentlessly and always find himself lacking. I realized Paul needed to hear "The Parable of the Distorted Lens."

The Parable of the
Distorted Lens

፨

You get into the driver's seat of your car; buckle up; start the engine and take off. It's all so automatic, isn't it? You've done it a million times.

You're driving along, and everything's fine. You look across to the passenger door rear view mirror, the one that's attached to the outside of the passenger door. What do you see?

You might see what's behind you. You would see if there is a car in the lane to the right, or perhaps you would see a part of the right side of your car, but what else would you see? What would you see every time you look in that particular mirror?

"OBJECTS ARE CLOSER THAN THEY APPEAR"

That's right. Those words are printed directly on that particular mirror. Most people forget that message when I ask them what they would see. We've seen it a million times. We know its there, but we don't remember it most of the time. Why are those words printed on that mirror?

Actually, the law requires it to be printed there. You see, the passenger door rear view mirror is curved. It is curved so that it gives the driver a wider angle view. You can see a wider area and, so, will be less likely to miss a car to the right of your car. However, there is a disadvantage to curving the mirror. It distorts reality. That curve in the mirror makes everything it reflects look smaller and thus farther away. Believing that a car in the right lane is farther back than it really is could cause us to pull over into the right lane too soon, cutting into the path of the car.

Let's look at some other examples. Have you ever tried on someone else's glasses? You put them on your face, and everything looks totally different. Things may become blurry or they may look bigger or smaller.

Have you ever been driving on a long trip and noticed some dark clouds approaching? You may have thought, "Man, that's a bad storm ahead." Then you remembered that you were wearing sunglasses. You lowered the sunglasses, and the clouds suddenly didn't look so dark and scary. Before you remembered the sunglasses, however, you believed you were seeing reality.

I'm sure you are familiar with the way that a lens changes what you see. It can make things look bigger, smaller, sharper, more blurry, or just distorted. It doesn't matter what you're looking at. The lens has the same effect on everything.

Once we become aware of the nature of our lens distortions, we can begin the work of correcting them. We do this by monitoring our perceptions as we go through our days and by catching ourselves whenever we see something that may come from our lens distortion.

As the rear view mirror illustrates, the distortion of a lens is consistent and, therefore, predictable. The writing on the mirror is always the same because the distortion of that lens is always the same. Objects in the mirror always appear farther away than reality, never appearing closer than reality. Your personal lens distortion is also predictable and consistent. This predictability of the distortion helps us in our efforts to correct it.

For example, if I know that my lens is distorted, such that I tend to see rejection, then I can learn to question any time that I feel rejected. I remind myself that this rejection perception or interpretation of an event is probably the result of my lens. I may even take it further, and make myself assume that I am accepted or liked by this person or group, rather than rejected.

You might ask, "So, what if you really are being rejected? What if they really don't like you?" I admit that is a possibility, but I would argue that I would find out eventually if they really were being rejecting.

If I assume they are being rejecting and they really aren't, I will probably never realize my misperception. If I assume they are rejecting me, my behaviors will change. I will probably distance myself. They may respond to my withdrawal by distancing themselves. I will then see their distancing as proof that I had been rejected in the first place. I would have created my reality from my expectations.

When I was a young boy, I liked Cracker Jacks. One of the attractions of Cracker Jacks was the toy or prize inside the box. I remember one simple prize that consisted of a 3 by 5 white card with many red and blue lines all over one side. It just looked like a scribbled mess, but the card also came with a piece of red cellophane and a piece of blue cellophane. When you put the red cellophane on the card, all the red lines disappeared and all the blue lines stood out. You could then see that those blue lines formed a picture. When you put the blue cellophane on the card, the blue lines disappeared and the red lines stood out. You could then see that the red lines formed a completely different picture.

Imagine that the Cracker Jacks card represents your life. The blue lines are the good things in your life. They depict your good characteristics, your abilities, or the good circumstances in your life. The red lines are the bad things in your life. They depict your negative characteristics, your weaknesses, or the failings in your life.

When you have sustained a wound of the heart, it is as if you subconsciously place a piece of blue cellophane on your life. The wound makes the good things about you or your life disappear. You don't notice those at all. It makes the bad things about you or your life stand out. Those are the things you pay attention to. Those are the things you remember. In your mind, those are the things that form the picture of your life. Of course, you don't realize that the blue cellophane is there, so you believe that you are seeing your life accurately.

In fact, you may have a loved one who asserts that there are many good things about you, but you dismiss those things as being unimportant or deny that the good things exist at all. You think to yourself that they are "just being nice" or "just trying to make me feel better."

Many of my patients have reported that they did have some people in their lives who communicated positive messages about their worth. Those people loved them and were good to them. They may have even gotten upset at other family members who mistreated them.

Whenever a child is exposed to some people who say she is not good enough and other people who say she is wonderful, her self-esteem is almost always formed by the negative message, not the positive. She will love the positive person but will tend to believe the messages of the negative person.

Sometimes our perception of reality is distorted by where we focus our attention. People have many things hitting their five senses at any moment. For example, right now you may be focusing your attention to the words on this page or you could focus your attention on one or more sounds in the room around you. You could focus your attention on something that is touching the skin on your foot or your arm. Many different things are contacting your senses, but you have to choose which ones will get your attention. When you focus your attention on one thing, the other things seem to disappear.

Applying the Parable

Learning to question our perception is a difficult task. We have spent our entire lives totally dependent on the assumption that our perceptions are an accurate reflection of reality. Acknowledging that we can't depend on those perceptions can be uncomfortable. It is, however, a necessary step toward seeing the truth. It's a bit odd that we hold on to the familiar, even when the familiar is very painful.

When my patients report some people who communicated negative messages about their worth and other people who truly valued them, I will have them do an exercise I call "Examining the Source." I ask them to name the people in their lives who were good to them. They give me the first names of people who communicated messages that they were worthwhile, capable and loveable. I write those names on the left side of my dry erase board under the word "Positive."

I then ask them to name the people who were negative toward them. They give me the first names of people who communicated through their words or behaviors that they were inadequate or unlovable or those that abused them. I write those names on the right side of the board, under the word "Negative."

After we complete the two lists of people, I ask the client several questions regarding each list. This "Consider the Source" exercise is in your homework for this chapter.

When my patients finish this exercise, they realize that the people who made them feel worthless or inadequate had their own problems. They see that those people said those things because such negative behavior was consistent with their character. My clients also realize that the people who made them feel loveable and competent were more trustworthy and emotionally healthy.

The following homework activities should help you identify distortions in your perception. Examine your lens. What reality distortions might your lens create? Consider the possible effect of your past experiences. Also, take a hard look at your day-to-day perceptions. What are your tendencies? Do you tend to magnify your failings while minimizing other's failings? Do you tend to minimize your own strengths and abilities while magnifying other's strengths? Do you magnify your own blame for negative life events? Are you a blame magnet?

Notice where you focus your attention. Do you tend to focus your attention on the negative circumstances in your life? Do the positive circumstances seem to disappear from your conscious awareness? Do you find that you mull over, analyze, and obsess about the negatives? Do you have Selective Attention?

1. Monitor your thinking for possible perceptual distortions. Identify any patterns. What are your tendencies? Complete the following sentences:

   A. When I think about myself, I tend to see myself as...

   _____

   _____

   _____

   _____

   _____

B.   When I think about my past, I tend to focus my attention on...

C.   When I think about my current circumstances, my tendency is to place more attention on...
     a.   The positive things in my life.
     b.   The negative things in my life.

D.   Because I realize I have a distortion in my lens and I now know the nature of that distortion, I will question my perception whenever I see....

E.   I will try to make myself assume the opposite of the above. This would mean that I would try to make myself assume that....

F.   Do the "Consider the Source" exercise on the next page. Spend some time thinking about your insights before you move on.

CONSIDERING THE SOURCE

Under "Positive about Me," write the names of those people (past and present) who have communicated positive messages about you through their words and behaviors. These people seemed to feel that you were worthwhile and/or competent. Under "Negative about Me," write the names of those people (past and present) who communicated negative messages about you through their words and behaviors. Some people may have communicated both positive and negative messages, but try to choose whether they were primarily positive or negative. If some people were equally positive and negative, you can write their name on both sides.

Positive about Me	Negative about Me

1. Which group do you trust the most?
2. Which group do you consider the most mentally healthy?
3. Which group do you like the most?
4. How do the people in the negative group treat most people?
5. Which group have you believed about who you are?
6. Write down negative personality traits or behavioral traits of the negative group members.
7. Were the negative people simply expressing those negative traits when they treated you negatively?

Concluding Comments:

It is not enough to realize that your perceptions are distorted. You must also know and understand the nature of the distortions. You need to understand your lens. If you know which misperceptions you tend to have, you can catch those misperceptions more easily and correct them. You can learn to see the events of your life more accurately.

It is difficult to accept that your perceptions are distorted. It is also hard to change those perceptions. The exercises above can help, but nothing can take the place of you monitoring your perceptions on a day-to-day basis.

Patients who use their journals on a daily basis have much more success at recognizing and changing their perceptual distortions. The format of the structured journal page will remind you to monitor your thinking and perceptions each day. It will also help you consider alternative perceptions.

My patients usually find the "Examining the Source" exercise to be quite enlightening. When they see the contrast between the people who have said negative things about them and those who said positive things, they display an immediate expression of recognition. For most, it is the first time they have thought of such a comparison. I think that you will find the exercise to be enlightening as well. You will see that those who hurt you most had significant problems and I think you will also realize that they hurt other people and not just you. Do you want to base your self-esteem on the messages of people who (1) you don't trust, (2) you do not consider mentally healthy, (3) you don't like, and (4) also treat others negatively? Do you want to allow those people to continue damaging your life?

A consideration of the side view mirror and other distorted lenses illustrates several truths. These are as follows:

1. Every human being sees himself or herself and the world through a lens.
2. When we are born, our lens is probably accurate.

3. Our experiences of childhood cause the lens to become distorted.

4. The severity of the lens distortion is determined by the severity of the negative childhood experiences.

5. The distortion of the lens tends to be consistent, producing the same distorted perceptions over time.

6. We have to understand the nature of our lens distortion and the perceptions it creates.

7. Lens distortions can cause Selective Attention where we magnify our faults or mistakes, while minimizing other's faults or mistakes.

8. Lens distortions can make us Blame Magnets, blaming ourselves for any problems we or our loved ones experience in life.

9. Being aware of our perceptual distortion tendencies and monitoring our daily thoughts for such distortions can help us correct them, thus decreasing the damage they cause.

Chapter 9
Treating Yourself with Compassion

Self-nurturing means, above all, making a commitment to self-compassion.
Jennifer Louden

The healing of a heart wound often requires several approaches. Each individual responds to one approach or technique better than another. In my practice, I try to give clients several tools to challenge their negative, dysfunctional thinking. They can then find the particular tools that they most relate to or that work best for them.

In this chapter, we will look at the emotional aspect of perception. Sometimes the facts of an event are quite evident. The seriousness of a mistake may be obvious as well. Sometimes a wound of the heart affects our attitude toward the mistake, and that can make all the difference.

When one has a wounded heart, he tends to have a harsh and unforgiving attitude toward himself. His mistakes or failures are often met with intense self-anger and frustration. The wound seems to create a "no-excuses" mentality that leaves little room for self-compassion. The wounded one withholds the kindness that he would show to any other human being with a similar failure. This was the case with one client named Jonathan.

Jonathan was a driven man. He was the Executive Director of a health care agency and was well-known in his small community. In addition to his formal job duties, Jonathan volunteered in several service organizations. Jonathan's greeting was always warm, cheerful, and professional. His employees described his management style as encouraging and kind. Despite his extremely busy schedule,

Jonathan seemed to have all the time in the world when an employee needed him.

I was familiar with Jonathan's positive reputation, so I was a bit surprised when he made an appointment to see me. He greeted me with the same warmth and kindness he showed everyone else. He even started the session by inquiring about how I was doing and how my practice was going. When I asked Jonathan how I could help him, his expression changed. He suddenly looked anxious and sad and reported that he made the appointment hoping to get rid of his panic attacks. He said he had been having them for about three months.

Panic attacks are characterized by a sudden rush of intense anxiety. The symptoms usually include racing and pounding heart, shortness of breath, muscles trembling, sweating, dizziness, and a feeling of unreality. The attack can cause the person to fear that they are going to die, going crazy, or that others will see the attack and they will be embarrassed. The attacks last a brief time. After they end the person may feel very tired or emotional.

Jonathan was having the panic attacks four or five times per week. He felt as if his life was getting out of control. He said that his attacks had forced him to excuse himself from two meetings and that he had cancelled several others. Jonathan also indicated that he had awakened several times in the middle of the night with a full-blown attack. As we talked he was able to identify the stressful event that triggered the attacks.

Jonathan indicated that he had made several "horrible" mistakes which had shaken his confidence. He had been responsible for preparation and submission of forms to renew a grant for a volunteer agency. He said he had confused the deadline date with a deadline on another project. Because of his error, the agency didn't get the grant. It was a small grant, but Jonathan described the mistake as "totally unacceptable." During the same month Jonathan completely forgot an important meeting. He said those at the meeting called him to see where he was and he was mortified with embarrassment. Finally, he said that he was overly harsh with two employees about mistakes they had made and that one of the employees later resigned from his agency. Of course, Jonathan blamed himself completely.

I asked Jonathan if anything had been different or more stressful prior to the month of mistakes. He responded with tears in his eyes that his grandmother died during that month. He said she had been his primary caretaker after his mother died at a young age, so she had been more like a mother to him.

I suggested that the death of his grandmother might have contributed to his month of errors, but Jonathan protested that trying to find excuses would be totally irresponsible. He muttered that he hated himself for being so incompetent.

I asked Jonathan if he had always tended to push himself, and he agreed that he did. He then added that pushing himself wasn't such a bad thing. Jonathan said he believed in striving for excellence. I agreed that we should all strive to do our best but questioned his harsh response to his mistakes. To illustrate my point, I told Jonathan "The Parable of The Good Coach and The Bad Coach."

The Parable of the
Good Coach and the Bad Coach

☙❧

Once there was a baseball player. He was a very good player. He was fairly good in the outfield, but he was particularly good at bat. This player was a power hitter, so he hit a lot of home runs. He had a good batting average overall, but he was particularly good at hitting home runs.

Unfortunately, there came a time when this player fell into a hitting slump. He would swing as hard as he could, but often he would strike out. The words would ring in his head, "Strike three. You're out!" The player occasionally would hit the ball; but even then he would hit a pop fly and be caught out, or he would hit a grounder and be thrown out at first. The player tried to figure out what he was doing wrong. He tried very hard, but he had been in this hitting slump for a while.

Tonight's game was particularly important as it would determine the team's chances for a playoff position. The player wanted so badly to hit the ball well, but he didn't. He struck out every time he came to bat. To make it worse, he was the last batter in the last inning. The player was the last out and the last hope. "Strike three!" His team lost the game.

One of his coaches marched up to him as he was coming off the field, and got right in his face. He yelled:

"You stunk out there! You're a waste of space on this team! I'm going to get rid of you as fast as I can figure a way to do it. I thought you had some talent, but you've got nothing! You look at that scoreboard. We lost this game, and you can put it on your shoulders because you sure didn't help us any tonight!"

The coach turned and marched off. The player didn't say anything but went back to the locker room. He showered and changed. As he was going to his car, hanging his head, one of his other coaches saw him. Now this coach had no idea what the first coach had done.

He approached the player saying:

"Hey, wait up. Get your head out of the dirt. I know you had a bad game. Fact is, you're in a pretty bad slump right now. But I know what you can do when you get hold of the ball. You have talent. You can kill the ball when you hit it. Slumps are made to be broken. We've just got to figure out what you're doing wrong. I want you to come an hour before regular practice tomorrow. I've got some videos of you hitting when you were doing well. I want to video your swing, and compare it to the ones I've got, so we can see what you're doing differently. Now go home and get some rest. Get your head up. You'll be okay! I'll see you tomorrow."

There are two coaches in this story. Coach A chewed him out when he came off the field. Coach B told him to meet him an hour early for batting practice. I have three questions for you.

Question 1:
Which of the two coaches would you say is the better coach? A or B?

Answer: _____

Question 2:
Which of the two coaches would you say has the best chance of helping this player pull out of his slump? A or B?

Answer: _____

Question 3:
Which of the two coaches are you to <u>yourself</u> when you mess up?
A or B?

Answer: _____

Applying the Parable

Most people have to admit that they usually act like the bad coach to themselves. Even though our logical minds know that the good coach would be more effective in helping us change, correct a bad habit, or perform better, we almost always treat ourselves as the bad coach would. We get angry with ourselves. We are harsh, even abusive to ourselves.

There was only one difference between the good coach and the bad coach. Both coaches recognized that the player was in a bad hitting slump. Both coaches recognized that the player could not continue the bad behavior and would have to pull out of his slump. The only difference was that the good coach approached the player with compassion, and the bad coach had none.

I realize that there may be times when a person may not be motivated, and confronting the behavior or even fussing at them may be helpful. Most people, however, are motivated to do better. They want to change but have trouble because they continually beat themselves down. They act like the bad coach to themselves most of the time. They feel inadequate and hopeless that they will ever be able to change.

Also, most people say that they would tend to be the good coach to someone else who messed up. When they encounter someone who has made a made a mistake and is being self-critical, they tend to be much more compassionate toward that person than they would be to themselves if they made the very same mistake.

The lower a person's self-esteem, the more he tends to act like the bad coach to himself. Often he will say things to himself in his mind which he would never think of saying to someone else who was down.

To be the good coach to yourself when you make a mistake, you need to:
A. Acknowledge the fact that you did make the mistake and the impact of the mistake.
B. Take responsibility for the mistake and the need to take corrective action.
C. Be compassionate or kind to yourself as you deal with the mistake.
D. Do not allow yourself to think any negative statement to yourself that you would not say if a loved one made the same mistake. Whenever you have a negative or self-critical thought about your mistake, ask yourself if you would say the same statement to a friend or loved one if they were in your shoes and felt the same way about the situation.
E. Ask yourself daily whether you are being the good coach or the bad coach to yourself. Strive each day to be the good coach to yourself. Let your experience be the proof that the good coach response is more effective in turning failures into successes.

Jonathan knew that the good coach would be more helpful to the baseball player, but admitted that he reacted to his own mistakes with the attitude of the bad coach. Sometimes, as he criticized himself during sessions, I would ask him if he was being the good coach or the bad coach. We then discussed how the good coach would have responded to the error or failing.

We also discussed how Jonathan would have approached an employee who made a similar mistake. He realized that he tended to be the good coach to everyone other than himself and readily admitted that his encouraging supervisory approach helped the agency employees perform at their best. Jonathan even recalled one department manager whom he had corrected because he tended to act like the bad coach when managing his staff. Jonathan recalled telling the manager that such criticism only served to destroy motivation and even quoted the joke poster, "The beatings at this company will continue until morale improves."

Jonathan began the habit of asking himself whether he was being the good coach or the bad coach to himself. He would often catch himself acting like the bad coach to himself and consider how the good coach would have responded. By treating himself as the good coach, Jonathan was gradually able to feel more energized and self-accepting. I think you'll find that this approach also works for you. I asked Jonathan to complete the following homework.

1.   Describe a mistake you have made or a failure you have experienced-something you are self-critical about.

_____

_____

_____

_____

_____

_____

_____

_____

_____

_____

2.   What "bad coach" statements did you make to yourself about that event?

_____

_____

_____

_____

_____

_____

_____

_____

_____

3.   What would the "good coach" say about this mistake?

_____

_____

_____

_____

_____

_____

_____

_____

_____

4.   Which statements (good or bad coach) would you say to a friend
      if he or she made the exact same mistake under exactly the same
      circumstances?

_____

_____

_____

_____

_____

_____

_____

_____

5.   This week pay attention to whether you are being the good
      coach or the bad coach to yourself. Make a daily note in your
      journal regarding your efforts to be the good coach to yourself.
6.   If you notice yourself being the good coach to someone else,
      think about why you did that for them but not for yourself.
7.   Use the Rubber Band Technique this week whenever you catch
      yourself acting like the bad coach to yourself. Try to replace
      each bad coach response with a good coach response.

Concluding Comments:

The tendency to react to our mistakes or failings like the bad coach seems to be fairly common. We often do that because we have a fear of being too easy on ourselves. We're afraid that if we let ourselves off the hook too easily we will become unmotivated and commit even worse failures in the future.

Addressing your mistakes or failures with compassion is an important aspect of perceptual change. When you look at your failings with compassion, you encourage yourself. You build up rather than tear down, engendering hopefulness rather than hopelessness.

Ask yourself several times each day whether you are being the good coach or the bad coach to yourself. Try to give yourself the same compassion that you would give anyone else who made the same mistake under the same circumstances.

The good coach and the bad coach have conveyed several truths. These are as follows:

1. Sometimes we really do make mistakes, and sometimes we really do fail.
2. Even when those mistakes or failings are serious, our attitude in addressing them is very important.
3. We can address our failures with harsh, no excuses, no forgiveness tones (the bad coach); or we can address them with compassion (the good coach).
4. Being compassionate with ourselves does not mean that we dismiss or underestimate the seriousness of our mistake. It doesn't mean that we are letting ourselves off the hook.
5. We know that the good coach's attitude simply works better in correcting failures and promoting later successes.
6. With daily practice and self-monitoring, you can learn to be the good coach to yourself.

Chapter 10
Learning to Judge Yourself Fairly

...Love your neighbor as yourself.
Matthew 22:39

In Chapter 9, you learned that addressing your mistakes with an attitude of compassion (the good coach) helps you heal your wounds of the heart. In this chapter, you will examine the impact of such wounds on your perception of those mistakes.

A wound of the heart creates an unfair bias against self. This bias leads you to apply one set of rules to the rest of the world and a different set of rules to yourself. During therapy sessions, I have often heard this bias played out. I have observed the unfairness of this attitude against self.

Healing the heart wound requires that you learn to treat yourself in a manner consistent with the way you treat others. Otherwise, the bias you hold against yourself will continually generate ammunition for self-abuse. Every mistake or failure will provide what you believe to be evidence of your core defect.

The Golden Rule states, "Love your neighbor as you love yourself." We often use that statement as a reminder that we should treat our neighbors well. While that is very true, there is another implication in the rule. It may help to break it down.

The statement consists of three parts. The first part is "love your neighbor." The second part is "love yourself." In between the two phrases is the word "as." This is a term of equality.

Imagine a balance scale with two pans suspended from a horizontal arm, which is balanced on a vertical arm. A balance scale is often used in images illustrating the balanced or equal stance of the law. Now imagine that the phrase, "love your neighbor" is on one pan, with the phrase "love yourself" on the other. In between is the word "as" meaning balance or equality.

The phrase literally means, "Love your neighbor to the same degree and in the same manner to which you love yourself." Some people do break the command by not treating their neighbors well. Others break the command by not treating themselves well.

Those with wounds of the heart tend to give others kindness and compassion, while not offering the same to themselves. They apply one set of rules, criteria or judgments to themselves, and another to the rest of the world.

I have had many patients who used this double standard, but Hannah stands out in my mind.

"I get so mad at myself when I...." You fill in the blank. Hannah used the phrase frequently. She judged herself without compassion or mercy.

Hannah was a fifty-six year old woman with a quick smile. She didn't look depressed when she first came in to see me, but I learned that Hannah held much sadness and anger behind that smile.

Her husband had left her when she was thirty-two, and she had not dated anyone since. Hannah's two children were grown, so she lived alone. She worked in an office but didn't enjoy her job.

Hannah was her own worst critic as she scrutinized her choices and behaviors and often found herself lacking. She had made several mistakes in her life, which she related readily. Her husband had left because she had an affair. Hannah said she didn't blame him for leaving her and that, "he should have done even worse," whatever that meant.

As we talked, she reported mistakes and failures in every area of her life. Hannah said she was a poor mother, that she disappointed her parents, and that she fully expected to be fired from her job at any time.

Hannah judged her mistakes as stupid and unforgivable and said she didn't deserve to be happy because of her poor choices. As Hannah described her failings, her facial expression could best be described as disgust.

As we talked about each mistake or failure, I asked Hannah if she knew anyone else who had made similar errors. She reported one friend who made a similar mistake, but Hannah's judgment of her was much less harsh. Hannah was very supportive of her friend, even though she disapproved of the affair. She encouraged the friend to forgive herself and move on.

I wanted to help Hannah see what she was doing to herself. She was quite surprised at my next statement.

The Parable of the Bigot

ॐ॰ॐ

"You're a bigot!"

The word itself sounds evil doesn't it? Even those who are truly prejudiced would feel insulted at being called a bigot. But are you prejudiced? If you bear a wound of the heart, I argue that you are, in fact, prejudiced. If you are denying being prejudiced, consider the following.

One is considered prejudiced whenever he or she pre-judges based on some identifying characteristic and without just grounds. Prejudice reflects an irrational attitude against an individual, a group, or a race. A prejudiced person perceives the targeted group or race in a negative light and, thus, perceives actions taken or underlying intentions of that group or race more negatively without sufficient cause.

Consider two examples. A prejudiced man is driving along a country road. He sees a man of his targeted race sitting on the side of the road in the grass. His thought may be, "That lazy so-in-so, he needs to get a job." About two weeks later, the same man is driving on a similar road and sees a man of his own race sitting on the side of the road in the grass. His thought might then be, "I wonder if he had car trouble." He observes the same behavior from both men, but the interpretation is totally different depending on race.

Let's look at another example. Once there was a judge presiding in a small town. One day while in his office he had two visitors from the state bar association. The visitors explained that they had come to talk to the judge about a problem in his court. The bar association had been reviewing sentencing patterns from judges across the state. When they reviewed his sentencing, they found that he had consistently handed down harsher sentences to black defendants, than he had to white defendants convicted of the same crimes.

The judge tried to argue against their accusation until he saw the printed evidence. There was a clear pattern that couldn't be denied. The bar representatives said that they would be monitoring his sentencing patterns over the next six months. If his prejudiced sentencing continued, he would be brought before the bar and probably lose his judgeship.

The judge didn't sleep very much that night. The next morning he entered his court with a determination to hand down equal sentences to defendants of all races. When a defendant of his targeted race was convicted, the judge asked himself what sentence he would have given to a defendant of his own race under similar circumstances. He then handed down that sentence to the defendant.

In each example, the prejudiced person judged one person more negatively than another simply on the basis of race. The man driving on the road made different assumptions about why the man was sitting on the side of the road. The judge was given a correct report of the defendant's behavior but rendered a more harsh punishment on the targeted defendants.

Now, do you see why you are prejudiced? Humm. You still don't get it? You see you are prejudiced against a rather small minority. It is a minority of one-you.

Think about how you judge yourself when you make a mistake or fail at something. How does that judgment compare with your judgment of someone else who made the same mistake or failed under the exact same circumstances?

If you have a wound of the heart, you are probably much harder on yourself than you are on others. You are probably much more compassionate toward others than you are on yourself. This is your bias. This is your prejudice.

If you can now admit that you are prejudiced against yourself, what do you plan to do to stop being such a bigot? Think about what the judge did. He imagined a defendant of his own race was standing before his bench. He asked himself how he would judge that person and forced himself to hand down a similar sentence. You can do the same.

Applying the Parable

What if you imagined putting someone else in your shoes? Imagine that someone else had made the same mistake under the same circumstances with the same information. Imagine that she felt as badly about the mistake as you feel. Imagine the person in your shoes is someone you like and respect. How would you judge her? What would you say to her? Would you even think the harsh thoughts about her that you have been thinking about yourself?

Doesn't it seem logical that the judgment she deserved for a particular behavior, mistake, or failure should be the same as the judgment you deserved? Shouldn't you show the same compassion to yourself that you would show them? I have personally tried to follow this technique for many years. I don't allow myself to judge my behaviors any more harshly than I would anyone else who did the same behaviors. I am no harsher on myself, and I am no more lenient.

This idea of using the same judgment on yourself that you would use on any other human being does seem perfectly logical, but here's where my clients run into a curious phenomenon. They truly believe that the rules that apply to all other human beings don't apply to them. They will counter my logical argument with statements like, "But I am different. I should have known better." They truly believe that they are different from all other human beings. They are exhibiting the Exclusion Delusion (see page 11).

A delusion is a symptom, usually of psychosis, where a person holds a belief that is clearly inconsistent with reality. If I believed that I was Napoleon, I would be delusional. If I believed that all people with blonde hair were terrorists, I would be delusional.

At this point in my career, I see very few clients who would meet the criteria for psychosis; but I have participated in the treatment of such disorders in the past. I never became accustomed to an encounter with someone exhibiting a psychotic process. Listening to someone, who was clearly out of touch with reality always seemed a bit unreal to me.

I have a very similar feeling when I listen to someone relate beliefs about himself or herself which are so clearly inconsistent with reality. Hearing the college professor question her intelligence; the kind and compassionate nurse and mother say that she is an "absolute waste of life;" or seeing the beautiful, young woman cry as she describes herself as ugly always takes me back a bit. I never quite get used to it.

Like any other delusion, a wound of the heart often causes the victim to believe himself or herself to be an exception to all the normal rules that apply to human beings. If I believe that I am different from every other human on earth, such that the rules that apply to others don't apply to me, then I am exhibiting the Exclusion Delusion.

So do you fit the definition of a bigot? Do you perceive your mistakes as more serious and judge yourself more harshly than you do others? If another person made the exact same mistake you made under exactly the same circumstances and felt the same remorse for the mistake would you judge them as harshly?

In order for a measuring device to be accurate it has to be consistent. If you had a scale that gave different readings when you repeatedly placed the same weight on it, it would be time to get a new scale. If a judgment is accurate, it should be consistent, regardless of who is being judged.

Hannah was quick to realize that she was prejudiced against herself. She realized that it was illogical to apply one set of rules for herself while she applied a different and more compassionate set of rules for everyone else. This realization was fairly easy for her when she looked at it.

The problem was that Hannah asserted that she had to be harder on herself. She stated her fear that she would become totally irresponsible and worthless if she didn't push herself. Hannah felt she needed the self-chastising to maintain her motivation and effort. I asked, "If this is true, then wouldn't everyone else also need to be chastised to maintain their motivation?" She didn't have an answer.

Hannah's thinking distortion can be illustrated by an old joke which I shared during our session.

A man walked into a bar holding his left hand above his head and wiggling his fingers. He stepped up to the bar and ordered a drink. The bartender said okay, but asked him why he was holding his left hand in the air. The man replied, "Oh that keeps the pink elephants away." The bartender said, "There are no pink elephants!" To which the man replied, "See, it works!"

As long as the man put his hand above his head, he wouldn't realize that the gesture wasn't needed to keep his pink elephants away. As long as Hannah chastised herself, she had no way of knowing that the chastising was unnecessary.

Hannah had to try judging herself in a manner that was equal to others before she realized that chastising wasn't needed. I asked her to try the technique of putting someone else in her shoes, and judging herself as she would judge them. At the next session, she reported that she had been able to practice the technique on one occasion. She said that she realized her bias against herself, but the exercise made her vaguely uncomfortable. She reported that her greatest discomfort was this nagging feeling that she was being too easy on herself.

With practice, Hannah gradually learned to use the comparison technique with regularity. Each time she put someone else in her shoes, judged herself similarly to the way she would have judged them, and experienced no negative consequences, she reinforced the technique. With this practice she found that she maintained her responsible attitude and, with time, her production actually improved due to her more positive mindset. She also realized that she could judge herself less harshly and still avoid inappropriate choices such as her earlier affair. I had Hannah do the following homework.

1. Recall a time when you made a mistake and were upset about the situation. Now think of some of the statements you made to yourself about that mistake.
    The Mistake: _____
    _____

    My Statements:
    _____
    _____
    _____
    _____
    _____

2. Now imagine that someone you like or trust had made the exact same mistake under exactly the same circumstances. Imagine that you said the statements you wrote

above to your friend after he made the mistake. How would you feel about saying those things to your friend? Write the statements as if saying them to your friend.

_____
_____
_____
_____
_____

3.   Think about the statements you would make to your friend, if he had made the mistake, and was feeling badly about it. Write them below:

_____
_____
_____
_____
_____

4.   Imagine saying those statements to yourself. How would those statements affect your mood or self-esteem?

_____
_____
_____
_____
_____

5.   How would you feel if you treated yourself as an equal to the rest of the world? Imagine the impact of your not being prejudiced against yourself. Write down some ways that you might be different if you were no longer biased against yourself.

_____
_____
_____
_____
_____
_____

Concluding Comments:

This is hard. I sit with my clients every day and watch them struggle. I see them go three steps forward and two steps back. Changing your perceptions of yourself will be some of the hardest work you will ever do. It will also be some of the most rewarding because it will be life changing. Don't give up. Work at it every day.

I recognize the similarities between this chapter and the last one on being the good coach. This is intentional. I find that each particular client relates well to one technique and not so well to another. One client connects to the story of the good and bad coach and finds that asking himself whether or not he is the good coach works well. Of course, the question has to be posed every day, perhaps for the rest of his life; but it works. Another client may relate well to the idea that she is prejudiced against herself. She is able to practice putting other people in her shoes and then applying her judgment of them to herself, and this works best for her.

You need to try all the techniques related in this book and then use them regularly. You will find that some techniques help you more than others.

In this chapter, a prejudiced driver and judge helped us with several truths. These are as follows:

1. A wound of the heart causes the bearer to be biased or prejudiced against self.
2. This prejudice makes the person judge himself more harshly than he would others who made the same mistakes or failures.
3. The prejudice also makes him interpret his behaviors in a more negative light.
4. The only way to stop the prejudice is to imagine someone else in his shoes and ask how he would judge that person. Then apply that judgment to himself.
5. You are a human being like every other human being. You should be judged equally with any other human being.
6. Practice loving yourself as you love your neighbor.

Chapter 11
Comparing Yourself to Others

I was always looking outside myself for strength and confidence but it comes from within. It is there all the time.
Anna Freud

Sometimes a wound of the heart alters the victim's perception in a way that makes everyone else look too good. Those who are wounded tend to see others as having it all together. They tend to assume that others don't share the insecurities they experience. They believe others feel competent and loved most of the time.

They may intellectually realize that this is not the case. When asked they will readily admit that many other people are hurting and that insecurities are common, but, in particular situations when they are feeling insecure, they will perceive those around them as being more self-assured, more competent, and more comfortable than they.

You may think it fortunate that others can't see your wound of the heart, but may not realize that it is even more unfortunate that you can't see the heart wounds in them. Since you can't see other's wounds, you are left with the assumption that your wound is unique or, at the very least, worse than that of those around you.

Of course, we all know people who are hurting. We know that tragedy comes to every life. We also know that others have self-esteem difficulties and that many deal with the scars left by neglect or abuse.

However, we tend to think of those things only when we are told the information or see it happening. Most of the time people present themselves as doing well or "having it all together." They work hard to present a positive image and, because they don't share their doubts, insecurities or pain, we assume those things are absent in their lives and present only in our own. Such an assumption can cause us to feel different, defective, or weak.

I have often heard statements such as, "Why don't others have the same problems that I have? Other people have bad things happen to them, but they seem to be able to get over it better than I. Maybe I'm just weak."

Everyone has some areas of insecurity. All human beings, regardless of their age, social status, position or income, have a little girl or a little boy inside them. It's that little girl or boy that is playful and fun loving. That is also the part of us that feels insecure and vulnerable.

When my patients share their stories and their reactions, I am able to see that inner child. I am able to see that the needs and vulnerabilities of the inner child are universal. I consider it an honor that my clients trust me with their story. In those sessions, they remove their usual social façade.

Adults have had many years to develop their façade. We learn to control our facial expressions and words. Our inner feelings are well hidden. Children often try to hide their feelings too, but they lack the skills to do it well. If you pay attention and know what to look for, the child's wound of the heart is apparent. Such was the case with one client, a little girl named Summer.

When I call patients out of the waiting room, it is natural for me to begin gathering information. Where they are sitting, how they are sitting, how quickly they get up out of the chair, and the way they approach me often provide important information. Do they make eye contact or avoid it? Does their facial expression suggest anxiety or sadness? How are they dressed?

Summer was twelve years old. She had pretty blue eyes, but I couldn't tell until later in the session as she kept her eyes focused on the floor. When I called her and her mother to come back for the appointment, she jumped as if she had heard gun fire. She held her mother's hand as we walked back to my office. Her face was a mixture of anxiety and sadness.

Summer's mother explained that the family had moved several times as Summer's father was in the military. Each time she had to start a new school which meant she had to be the new kid once again. Through the years, she had become more and more withdrawn.

This year her grades had dropped significantly, and her teacher expressed concerns about her sad countenance and extreme withdrawal from her classmates. Summer's pain was getting worse.

In the beginning of the session, Summer's mother answered all my questions. The only responses I received from Summer were nods of her head with eyes facing downward.

I asked Summer if I could talk to her for a bit while her mother waited in the waiting room. She hesitated but nodded yes after some urging from her mother.

I began by offering to show Summer some of the various items in my office. My office is filled with artifacts from my travels. I try to have some items of interest for all ages. Summer followed me around the room as I told a brief story about each item. Her comfort level gradually increased.

I told Summer that I liked to talk to children because I often get to sit on the floor while we talk. I said that adults usually don't like to sit in the floor and talk to me and asked her if she would like to sit on the floor while we talked. She said she would and sat down.

When I felt she was ready to talk, I asked her why she thought she felt uncomfortable around her classmates. She looked down and said, "I'm just different from everybody else." Now, we had a beginning.

As our talks progressed, Summer expressed the belief that she didn't think or feel like everyone else. She said they all seemed to be happy and to be having fun. She said she didn't talk much because she was afraid others would think she was weird or odd and laugh at her. She said that she wished she could just be like everyone else.

I told Summer that I wanted to tell her "The Parable of the Secret."

The Parable of the Secret

కొళ్ళ

Once there was a land that was very far away. The people were much like the people here. They were born, grew up, worked, married, and had children. They interacted in much the same ways that people interact here.

There was one interesting difference in this land though. Whenever a baby was born in this land, she was born with a small chest like a treasure chest. The chests looked like the treasure chests you may have seen, with a lid that closed and a lock. All people were born with their own individual chests. Everyone, of course, knew that everyone else had a chest; but only the owner of a chest could open it up and look in it. Only the owners could really know the contents of their chests.

In this land, it was common for people to mention some of the items in their chests when conversing over dinner or while walking along together. Sometimes a comment about an item in one's chest might be added, if it pertained to the topic of conversation. It was all pleasant enough.

There was this one girl in the land who was troubled by her chest. The chest itself didn't bother her. The contents did. When the girl became old enough, like everyone else, she opened her chest and examined the contents. She found some very beautiful things in her chest. She found some neutral things, but she also found some things that weren't beautiful at all. In fact, they were ugly. These things made her sad.

The girl listened as other people commented on the contents of their chests. She listened as they spoke of beautiful things or interesting things. She paid attention when they would share some of the neutral things in their chest. She listened for mention of ugly things like those contained in her chest. There was no mention of such.

The girl never told anyone about the ugly things in her chest. She tried to not think about them herself. She would sometimes push the ugly things to the bottom of the chest and cover them up with neutral or beautiful things, but she knew they were down there. She still knew.

She sometimes kept her chest lid closed for long periods of time; but every time she glanced at the chest, she knew the ugly things were in there. Again she felt sad.

The girl had a fear that somehow others would be able to know about the ugly things in her chest. She said fewer words for fear that she would give it away. The girl felt different and ashamed. She kept to herself more.

One day the girl was walking on a dirt road outside of town. She often walked there because she could be alone, and she liked to be alone. The girl was particularly sad that day as she was pondering why she had such ugly things in her chest.

Suddenly the girl was startled by the realization that she was no longer alone. An old man was walking beside her on the road. The girl hadn't noticed him approaching. He just seemed to be there.

He was an odd-looking old man with long scraggly hair and a long white beard. His clothes were simple and somewhat disheveled. He made her nervous.

She walked faster, thinking that she could distance herself from the man, but he walked faster as well staying beside her.

She slowed down then, thinking she would let him move on; but he slowed down as well and stayed beside her.

She was then even more nervous when he spoke to her and said, "What's the matter?"

She said, "Nothing," and walked faster; but he kept pace.

He then said again, "What's the matter?" And there was something kind in his voice, so she found herself talking to this old man. Perhaps because he seemed kindly enough or possibly because she figured she would never see him again, she shared her private story.

She began to explain that she had found ugly things in her chest, things that made her ashamed. She wondered aloud why she had to be different. She said she had always wished that she didn't have the ugly things-that she could have a more normal chest. The girl stared at the dirt road as she walked and talked.

When she finished, the girl looked over at the old man for his response. He was grinning this big, toothless grin. She was immediately angry.

"Here I have told you something I have never shared with anyone, and you're laughing at me," she blurted.

He kept walking and responded in his kindly voice, "I'm not laughing at you at all. I'm smiling, because I know something you don't know."

A little calmer, she asked, "Like what?"

He responded, "You wouldn't believe me if I told you. This truth you have to discover for yourself, but when you return to town, pay attention to the people you meet. Listen to them when they're talking. Really listen. Spend more time thinking about them and less time worrying about what they might be thinking about you. Listen between the lines. Listen when they don't know you're listening. Really listen and you'll discover what I know."

The girl turned to ask him another question, and the old man was gone. He was nowhere to be found- just gone. After the shock wore off she went home. The girl pondered her experience with the old man and wondered what he knew that was so important. Then she began to follow his advice.

The girl listened to those around her. She focused her attention on others rather than being so self-conscious. After a while she realized that it is impossible to be self-conscious and other-conscious at the same time. When she was self-conscious, she was not really aware of others. When she was truly focused on others, she lost all sense of self-consciousness.

She began to see hints of what the old man was talking about. Then she felt more certain. And then the girl knew. She knew what he was talking about. She knew what made him smile.

You see, the old man knew that everyone's chest was alike. Everyone had good things, neutral things, and ugly things in their chest. Everyone just talked about the good or neutral things, but the ugly things were in their chests, just like hers.

From that time forth, the girl felt better. She realized that she was normal. She realized that she was like everyone else, but that wasn't her most important lesson. She had learned to focus her attention on others. In doing so, the girl became less self-conscious. She belonged.

Applying the Parable

I often tell my clients that I feel truly blessed to be able to do what I do. I get to spend my time helping people. I get to see people change their lives. I even get to participate in a small extent in that change.

One of the major blessings of being in a counseling practice is my unique window on the world. People come into my office and talk to me about things that they never tell another soul. They reveal their inner thoughts, their fears, and their insecurities. They remove the mask they wear most of the time. My clients allow me to see behind the wall; and as they do, I realize something very important. I get to see how much we human beings are alike. We all have hopes, fears, insecurities, weaknesses, and strengths. We all wonder if others would accept us if they knew what went on in our head. It is a very comforting assurance to see the similarities that all human beings share-that everyone has good and bad stuff in their chest.

I wish I could say that the story had an immediate impact on Summer, but that was not the case. She didn't react at all to the story at first. We talked about the meaning of the story, and she understood it well. Her hesitancy was because she didn't believe the moral of the story to be true. She said that the other kids just looked as if they were happier than she. She said that they all seemed to like each other. She believed her observations to be true.

To break through her perceptions, I asked her to name specific classmates. She gave me their names and where they sat in class. We then went through each one while I asked her questions. With specific questioning, she was able to relate an awareness of difficulties that some of those children experienced. She related that this one seemed shy or that that one talked badly about his parents. She was able to identify some children who seemed unpopular. Gradually, by taking a closer look at each classmate, she was able to realize that others did share some of her concerns.

I then asked her to pay attention to the other children when she returned to school. I asked her to look for evidence that their "chest" had things that were similar to hers. In fact, we made it into a game where she received points for every piece of evidence she observed.

Summer's mother agreed to ask the teacher to recommend some girls she could invite to go to a movie with Summer. She later arranged a sleepover with some girls who had been particularly nice to Summer. Afterward, we discussed her thoughts about those girls and how they had many feelings that were similar to hers. Over time, her mood improved. Toward the end of our sessions, she told me about a girl that was new to the class. She said she had befriended the girl to try to help her feel better because she knew how she felt. I just nodded in agreement, but I knew that Summer now understood!

While this story was written for children, they certainly are not the only ones who need it. Adults are just as prone to assume that they are unique in their insecurities and pain. I remember a therapy group I facilitated for individuals with Panic Disorder. The members had experienced panic attacks for anywhere from six months to eleven years. The first session was surprising and fascinating.

I began by introducing myself and having each group member introduce himself or herself. I described the symptoms of a panic attack and invited the group members to share their experiences with each other. That's when it began.

You would have thought the group members were long-lost relatives at a family reunion. They compared experiences, supported each other, and discussed how panic attacks had impacted their lives. They smiled and they cried. Most of all, they expressed a relief and comfort that they had found others who shared their condition. They no longer felt alone.

Prior to this first group session, most of the participants had not shared their experience with anyone outside their immediate family. If they had shared, they were met with supportive words but only a partial understanding since others couldn't really understand a panic attack without having had one. Some group members had not shared with another soul prior to that night.

The homework below is designed to help you to see the similarities between yourself and others. My hope is that you can feel the comfort of knowing that you are not alone.

1. During the next few weeks, try to follow the old man's advice. Notice other people. Really observe them. Try to listen with the goal of understanding them. Every person has a story. Everyone you meet is human with all the strengths and weaknesses of being human. Try to remind yourself that they work to present an acceptable façade just as you do. In your journal, note your observations of other's human vulnerabilities. Make notes of any ways that they are similar to you.

2. If you do the first assignment for a few weeks, you will begin to notice yourself feeling less self-conscious. Try to remind yourself that others are just like you. Remind yourself that they are not scrutinizing you. After all, do you spend your time scrutinizing others? Assume that those around you have their story and try to imagine it. You will need to do this repeatedly, day-after-day, before it will begin to seem believable. With persistence, however, you will begin to see that it is true.

3. Remind yourself that everyone you meet has experienced pain and loss. Life is wonderful, but life is also difficult. Troubles are visited upon everyone. Once we accept that, we can let it go and move on. Know that you are not alone.

4. The next time you stop at a stoplight, notice the faces of the people driving across in front of you. Consider that each one has a story. Ask yourself what may be going on in each life. Think about what things are good about their lives and what things are bad. What are their insecurities? What are their struggles? What are their triumphs? Like you, each has a story. You can practice this little mind game any time you are in a place where you can observe others such as a mall or at church. Doing so will reinforce the truths of the story.

5. In the space below, write the first names of ten people you know. These can be friends or co-workers or family

members. In the right hand column, write some vulnerability or insecurity you have sensed in them or some tragic or painful event they have experienced.

People I know: Their vulnerability or painful event:

1. _____
2. _____
3. _____
4. _____
5. _____
6. _____
7. _____
8. _____
9. _____
10. _____

When you consider the people on the list above and their vulnerabilities, do they seem more similar to you or more different? Remember that you only know a portion of their vulnerabilities or insecurities. Every person on the list has his own story. You only know a part of that story. When we see behind the façade, we realize how much we are like others.

Concluding Comments:

I wrote "The Parable of the Secret" specifically to help children understand that they are more like others than they realize. The story is childlike, and sometimes I think about writing one with more of an adult theme. Then I remember that we all have that little boy or girl inside us, and I leave the story alone.

The point of this story is an important truth and such a comforting one. When we learn to see other humans as vulnerable creatures like ourselves, we become so much more comfortable in our skin. We become less self-conscious. This allows us to become more other-conscious, which allows us to more clearly see the vulnerabilities in others. Again, remember that it is impossible to be self-conscious and other-conscious at the same time. When you are being self-conscious, you are focusing your attention on how others see you.

You can't really observe them. If you are being other-conscious, you will tend to forget yourself and your concerns about how others view you.

To see the vulnerabilities, the strengths, the weaknesses, and the insecurities in others you only have to look, but you have to really look. You have to be able to see under the façade. You have to look with the expectation that you will see those vulnerabilities!

The strange old man revealed some important truths. They are as follows:

1. We are well aware of our own negative thoughts, our insecurities and our failings.
2. We work to hide our "weaknesses" from others. We want to appear as if we are doing well and "have it all together." We often succeed in doing that.
3. We assume that others are doing well and that they don't have the insecurities and doubts that we have.
4. Because of these assumptions, we feel different from others. We feel isolated or alone.
5. When we are self-conscious, we cannot be other-conscious. When we are other-conscious, we cannot be self-conscious.
6. We sometimes fear that others wouldn't like us if they really knew us.
7. The truth is that every human being has doubts, insecurities, or weaknesses.
8. It is comforting to know that we are like others rather than different.

Part 3
Persistence

By now I'm sure you have realized the difficulty inherent in this work. The negative beliefs you formed during childhood were so deeply engrained. You developed beliefs about who you are, who you are not, where you fit in, and where you do not. The fact that those beliefs were lies didn't lessen their impact. Those beliefs have altered your life without your knowledge. They have infected your day-to-day experience and created insecurity, anxiety, depression, anger, and pain.

The infection of negative self-esteem beliefs can be compared to a metastasized cancer. A metastasized cancer has spread into surrounding tissue and has become integrated into that tissue. The damage inflicted by the cancer gradually spreads throughout the body. If it is not destroyed by surgery, chemotherapy, or radiation, the cancer will eventually kill the body.

Like cancer, your self-esteem beliefs have become integrated into every area of your life. Every event that happens to you, every relationship in your life, your thoughts, moods and attitudes are all affected by your beliefs about yourself. This metastasis makes recognizing and changing those beliefs very hard.

Recognizing and changing your negative self-esteem beliefs requires persistence. You will have to be persistent in monitoring your thinking and perceptions. You will have to be persistent in using the tools you have been given in this book. This is a life-long task. We all have to continue to work on our beliefs for all of our lives. As you practice this the work gets easier; but it remains necessary, and it continues to be work.

Your persistence in this work requires more than repetition. It requires that you apply these ideas to every area of your life. Each chapter in Part 3 is designed to help you apply this work to an important area of your life. Some chapters will apply generally and some will be very specific in their application. Some chapters may address areas that you haven't experienced (for example, sexual abuse), but you can still gain from reading them.

You're coming into the home stretch. Keep reading. Don't give up. Don't assume you have it beaten. Don't let your guard down. Those self-esteem lies will slip back into your brain and your life before you know it. Be diligent in your work. You are worth it! Your life is worth it!

Chapter 12
Overcoming Helplessness

No man is ever whipped until he quits—in his own mind.
Napoleon Hill

At some point during the process of healing a wound of the heart, most people will experience a feeling of hopelessness or helplessness. The quest to overcome a lifetime of negative thinking can be totally overwhelming. Most clients will experience good days when they are able to think more positively followed by days when their thinking is as negative as ever. Their moods will fluctuate accordingly. When a period of improved thinking and mood is followed by a return to negative thinking, the person may conclude that the perceived improvement was "just a fluke" and that they are "back to square one."

During my early training, I was taught the importance of predicting "a temporary setback" in a client's improvement. I was taught to tell the improving client that they should expect some temporary setbacks where they return to the old feelings or old symptoms. A setback often does occur during the process of recovery. If the client isn't forewarned about this event, he may conclude that he is back to square one and that the improvement wasn't real. When he makes this conclusion, the setback can be prolonged and worsened. I help the client understand that he is simply experiencing a temporary setback so that he will not be shaken by the experience, and the setback will pass fairly quickly.

In discussing temporary setbacks, I compare the client's course of recovery to a graph of the stock market. Such graphs may show that the market value has grown over time, but that growth is marked by many gains and losses. It isn't a smooth growth. Neither is the client's improvement. Your improvement won't be smooth. You will experience ups and downs. You should expect temporary setbacks. Try to keep this perspective so you won't feel hopeless or helpless when those setbacks occur.

For some, however, feelings of helplessness or powerlessness are constant companions rather than occasional visitors. Such feelings can sometimes be traced back to childhood experiences. The negative experiences of childhood can foster an overall perception of helplessness. Those helpless feelings return later when the adult faces adversity. The child learns to perceive herself as powerless. Without intervention, that perception tends to linger into adulthood.

When a child is surrounded by adults who love her and care for her, she learns to feel safe. As she grows, those adults gradually give her more independence and power to direct her life. As a result, she feels more empowered, competent, and independent.

When a child is surrounded by adults who are controlling, smothering, abusive or anxious themselves, she feels unsafe and learns to feel helpless. As she grows, she continues to feel helpless and powerless. For that child, the world seems like a dangerous place, and she feels incompetent to deal with it.

Children have a natural tendency to feel powerless and helpless. After all, they are. They are truly at the mercy of the adults who surround them. This is the reason those adults have such a major impact on the child's psychological development.

There is an old concept in psychology called "locus of control." It means "location of control" and a person is said to have either an internal or an external locus of control.

A person with an internal locus of control perceives that she has primary control over what happens in her life. She believes that her behaviors and choices determine whether good or bad things happen to her. It's an attitude of "if I want it badly enough, I can make it happen" or "my life will be what I make it to be."

A person with an external locus of control perceives that the environment has primary control over what happens in her life. She may hope that good things will happen but tends to feel that her behaviors or choices have a very limited influence over the outcomes in her life.

In the 1967 a psychologist named Martin Seligman introduced the concept of Learned Helplessness. His research demonstrated that we can learn to perceive ourselves as helpless, even when we are not actually helpless. This can happen when we have endured earlier situations where we have truly been helpless and could not stop or prevent painful events. People who have been helpless in their early lives can later perceive themselves to be helpless, even when they aren't.

When children are abused or mistreated, they are truly helpless. They don't have the power to stop the pain. Later in their lives, as adults, they may perceive themselves to be helpless to change their life situations, even when they have the power to do so. Many times they endure painful situations for years without even attempting change.

During her first session, Anna reported that her husband left her when she confronted him about his affair. With no apologies, he quietly packed his bags and moved out. Two weeks later she was laid off from her job. Anna knew that unemployment benefits alone wouldn't cut it. She simply wondered how long it would be before she lost her apartment. She was emotionally paralyzed, and she was depressed.

During our early sessions, Anna expressed her grief, anger and fear. While her physical stature was about average, she appeared to shrink as she sat on the couch. She fiddled with her fingers and focused her eyes on the floor.

In one session, Anna reported that she had gone to visit her mother the previous weekend. She said she had hoped to get some emotional support but added that she should have known better.

Many times people remind me of the Peanuts comic strip where Charlie Brown keeps trying to kick the football while Lucy holds it. She always pulls it away him, and he always falls on his back, but he continues to try. Often, people go back to that critical or neglectful parent with a hope that, maybe this time, they will receive a positive response. Time-after-time they are disappointed, and their old negative beliefs about themselves are strengthened. They want that positive response from the parent so badly that they keep going back.

Anna reported that during this visit, her mother was critical of her, just as she had been during her childhood. Her mother even said at one point, "No wonder you couldn't keep a husband." Anna's beliefs seemed confirmed.

There was one therapeutic benefit to Anna's difficult trip home. While there, she was able to identify an additional feeling that she had experienced while growing up and that she still tends to experience today- a deep sense of helplessness or powerlessness.

Anna remembered that she had felt the same feelings throughout her childhood; but more importantly, she indicated that she experiences that state of mind today whenever she considers making positive changes in her life. It was a "what's the use" kind of feeling, and it made her want to give up and stay in bed. I told her that her feelings reminded me of a story.

The Parable of the
Elephant's Deception

૭૰ન૬

There was great excitement and commotion when the circus came to town, especially in this small town. Nothing much happened here-same routine day after day, but this day was special. The circus was coming to town!

These events happened a long time ago, so this was an old fashioned circus that was held in a big canvas tent. As the circus paraded into town in brightly painted wagons, a small band played music. Clowns danced around greeting the people and handing out candy. Some wagons carried exotic animals.

The little girl's eyes were wide as she studied each part of this spectacle, but she was particularly fascinated by the largest of the creatures. The elephant was huge with rough, wrinkled, gray skin. It moved slowly, and its small eyes seemed to be studying the people as it passed by. She had never seen anything like it.

The little girl wasn't aware that she had been following the elephant down the parade route, weaving in and out of the crowd. She stayed with it as far as she could. Something about this creature captured her attention.

It was hard to go to sleep that night. The little girl kept replaying the parade scene in her mind, but most of all, she kept picturing the elephant's eyes. They seemed too small for its head and body, but that wasn't what interested her. They looked sad. Now, I don't know how one tells when an elephant looks sad, but nonetheless, she saw sadness in those eyes.

The next morning she awoke early, got dressed, and headed out to the field to watch the circus people setting up. In truth, she was only interested in seeing one creature. There were already other people watching, but they were kept at some distance by a boundary of metal pipes sticking in the ground with a long yellow ribbon circling the field.

The girl circled the entire ribbon fence trying to get another look at the elephant, but the many wagons and the large tent already partially erected kept it out of sight.

Even while her little hand was lifting the yellow ribbon, she couldn't believe she was doing what she was doing. She wasn't the type of girl who would go against the rules, but here she was sneaking under the barrier and into the forbidden area where the circus set-up was taking place. She was able to avoid being noticed as she walked slowly beside some of the wagons. Then she saw what she was looking for.

The elephant seemed to be swaying slightly as it stood in a little clearing. It had lifted some hay in its trunk and was chewing slowly. There was a large, leather band attached to a thick rope around one of its ankles. The rope was attached to a wooden stake, which had been driven into the ground. Then she focused in on its small eyes. They still looked sad. They didn't seem to be looking at anything in particular, but they definitely looked sad. She sat down on a tuft of grass, propped her head in her hands and watched the elephant eat.

She didn't hear anyone approaching, so she was startled when a hand touched her on the shoulder. Her head spun around to see one of the workers standing right behind her looking down. He looked pretty old to her, but then most adults did. His clothes were dirty. He had gray hair, a scruffy moustache, and faded tattoos on both fore-arms.

She fully expected to be fussed at, but his voice was kind and soft as he commented, "She's beautiful isn't she?" The only sound she could make was, "Uh huh." Then he sat down beside her on the grass.

He joined her in watching the elephant as he questioned, "Do you see how she's attached to that rope and stake?"

She said, "Yes."

He continued, "She's a mighty large creature, and she's very strong. Did you know that she could easily pull that stake out of the ground and go wherever she wanted to go? "

The girl asked, "So why doesn't she?"

"When she was first born, her owner put a band around her an-kle and tied her to a rope and stake just like this one. At that time she was much smaller and weaker so she couldn't pull the stake out. She wasn't strong enough. They have kept her tied to that rope all of her life. As she grew up, she became strong enough to pull the stake out; but she never tried to. She had learned when she was little that she was helpless to pull free, and she still believes she is helpless to pull free now, even though she's not."

"That's so sad," whispered the little girl.

"Yep," responded the man.

"Is that why her eyes look so sad?" she asked.

"Don't know much about that," he noted, "but I guess it could be. But, right now, we had better get you out of here, before both you and I get into trouble."

Applying the Parable

"I can't do that." "I'm not smart enough to go to graduate school." "I so wish I could change jobs, but I don't know how to do anything else." "Who would hire me?" "I'm a failure." "I'm a loser." "I've always been this way." "You can't change the way you've thought all your life!"

In my practice, I charge a fee for counseling sessions, but the fee is not my actual payment. The fee enables me to earn a living, support my family, and not have to work at another job. The fee allows me to spend my time doing counseling rather than something else; but the actual way that I get paid is seeing people change, seeing people get better.

I get a personal satisfaction from seeing an individual become empowered. I enjoy being a part of the process as a depressed individual recovers or an anxious person becomes more calm and secure.

Everything I do as a psychologist is based on the belief that people can change. I know this as more than a belief because I see it happening every day. I have the privilege of witnessing it first hand. I consider myself to be truly blessed to do so.

At this point, I can't resist telling my favorite psychologist joke. Here it is. "How many psychologists does it take to change a light bulb?........Just one, but the light bulb has to really want to change."

Okay, so I won't be able to support myself as a comedian, but people can change. They have to really want to do it, but they can.

Anna's eyes were tearful when I finished the elephant story. She said that she had felt like the elephant all her life. She said she would love to feel that she had the ability to change. She commented that she was tired of feeling helpless.

In the next session, I worked with Anna on setting goals. I asked her to imagine she could do anything she wanted. Her first goal was simply to get her house cleaned up. She set up a schedule to get a certain, reasonable amount completed each day until the task was done. She set up several other immediate goals which seemed reasonable.

We then worked on Anna's making broader changes. She said she would like to attend the local community college but had thought that to be an impossible goal. Despite the fact that Anna made good grades in high school, she didn't think she had the intelligence to succeed in college.

Of course, Anna's progress came in small steps. She had several setbacks during our work together, but with encouragement, she persisted. Each time she succeeded in a goal, her feeling of helplessness faded.

Anna gradually decreased frequency of sessions and then discontinued therapy. I ran into her about two years later. She said that she had completed a nursing degree and had a job at a local hospital. She was dating someone, and reported the relationship to be going well so far.

During our counseling, I asked Anna to do the following homework.

1. Make a list of some of the negative or painful circumstances you experienced during childhood but were absolutely powerless to change:

   a. _____

   b. _____

   c. _____

   d. _____

   e. _____

   f. _____

2. Would any other child of the same age have been able to change those circumstances?

3. Now list some of your current circumstances that you would like to change:

a. _____
b. _____
c. _____
d. _____
e. _____
f. _____

4. Have you felt helpless or powerless to change these current circumstances? Is it possible that your perception of helplessness is based on your childhood experience rather than your current reality? Is it possible that you could change those circumstances if you simply felt empowered to do so?

5. This week, notice any thoughts or actions that would suggest that you are being held back or held down by self-limiting beliefs. Write them down below:

_____
_____
_____
_____
_____
_____

6. If you knew you had the ability and the power to accomplish anything, what would it be? What are your dreams? What were your past dreams?

_____
_____
_____
_____
_____
_____

7. Now, develop some specific, more immediate goals. These can be short-term or long-term goals. They should

be written in terms such that anyone could tell whether the goal had been met or not. Your goals should also have a time frame. For example, a goal of "I will complete a degree in nursing" is not as effective as, "I will complete an RN degree by January 1, 2013." Write your goals below.

Goal:

_____
_____
_____
_____
_____
_____
_____

Time Frame:
This week, try saying the following statements, or something similar, to yourself several times per day, and see how it makes you feel.

1. "As a child, I was helpless. I am now an adult and I can change my life."
2. "If anyone else can do it, I can do it too."
3. "I can do anything if I set my mind to it."

Concluding Comments:
Feeling empowered to make changes and feeling a sense of control in life is a very gradual process, but setting goals and taking action helps. Most of the steps in healing a wound of the heart require a change of perception. Overcoming helplessness also requires action. You don't feel truly empowered until you take action and see the proof for yourself. It takes time and persistent effort to rid yourself of the perception of helplessness.

From the circus elephant, we learned the following truths:

1. When you were young, you truly were helpless and powerless.

2. As you grew up, you became stronger and more capable of making changes in your life.

3. You didn't realize this and assumed you were still helpless.

4. You now have the power to make changes in your life.

5. You can now do whatever you need to do to make your life better!

6. In order to do this, you may have to start with small choices or actions, and work your way up to the bigger changes.

7. Your efforts will be more effective if you write down specific goals and develop a plan to achieve those goals.

Seligman, M.E.P.; Maier, S.F. (1967). "Failure to escape traumatic shock". *Journal of Experimental Psychology* 74: 1–9.

Chapter 13
Learning to Take Care of Yourself

If you don't run your own life, somebody else will.
John Atkinson

In the last chapter, you learned that a wound of the heart can cause its victim to feel helpless and powerless. Recognizing this fact and taking action will help you conquer the perception of helplessness, but then you encounter another problem.

A heart wound can also cause the individual to devalue his own opinions, desires, and values. He places little importance on his own desires. He is not assertive regarding what he wants. He may not even be aware of what he wants.

A starving person will actually lose his hunger drive when enough time has passed without eating. When given food he may refuse to eat or eat very little. In the same way, when a person has gone a long time without thinking about or asserting himself concerning his wants, he may lose touch with those wants altogether. If given an opportunity to state what he wants, he may be unable to come up with anything.

When food becomes available to the starving person, he must consume very small amounts at first. He can then gradually increase the intake of food. After a time, he will regain his healthy appetite. In the same way, the person who has lost touch with his own desires or opinions can gradually get in touch with those desires by being assertive, first about small matters, and then larger matters.

Unfortunately, the wound can also cause the victim to place an inordinate value on the opinion of others. The approval or disapproval of others takes on a greater importance. Decisions are based on the anticipated reactions of the observing others. The internal question, "What would they think?" becomes the compass because the victim has lost touch with his own compass. A life ruled by the opinions of others is a life half-lived.

Is it possible for a child to be too good? What is the cost of over-compliance? What does one lose when one loses control over his life's direction? I recall one client, Andrew, who was familiar with such a loss.

His physician had correctly diagnosed Andrew with moderate depressive disorder. He referred him to me because his symptoms had been resistant to treatment. During the first session, Andrew described his history. He said that he was an only child. With a weak smile, he described his parents as "wonderful" and described his childhood as "ideal." Andrew described his current life, however, as "empty and lonely."

Andrew knew that he felt unhappy but didn't understand why. He said that he had never married and that he lived alone in an apartment. Andrew had worked as a school teacher for fifteen years, but admitted that he had never really liked teaching. Both of his parents were school teachers, and it was always understood that he would follow in their footsteps.

With further prompting, he noted that his parents were very loving and supportive, but they parented in a clearly authoritarian manner. He knew better than to challenge them. Andrew remarked that he never had a rebellious stage, as he always complied with his parent's wishes. He added that he rarely had to be punished as a look of disapproval was usually enough to put him back in line.

As we talked further, Andrew admitted that his parents could be intimidating when they corrected him. He also admitted that he sometimes felt an overwhelming tension in the home.

During one session, Andrew recalled a childhood moment which seemed to be important. He said that he could see himself standing stiffly in the middle of a room with his arms held down by his sides. He said that it seemed he stood there for a very long time, almost paralyzed, afraid to move in any direction. He couldn't remember details, but said he thought his parents had gotten upset with something he had done. Andrew remembered the fear that he would do something else to upset them, so he didn't move.

Andrew commented that he loved to write but hadn't taken the time to do so in several years. He had published a poem and a couple of short stories but said they weren't a big deal. His parents told him there was no future in writing and that he needed a secure job; so he followed their wishes and taught school like them.

Andrew had never dated much, and his last date was in college. There had been one relationship with a girl named Jennifer which lasted about two years. He said he truly loved her but that it would have never worked out, as she had strong opinions and had openly disagreed with his parents on more than one occasion. His parents convinced him to end the relationship. He heard that Jennifer married a few years later. As he spoke, I could see that he was still grieving the loss.

I told Andrew that I was reminded of a client I had seen many years ago who taught me an important lesson. I went on to tell him "The Parable of the Life Lived for Others."

The Parable of the
Life Lived for Others

৵৽৽

About twenty years ago I was asked to do a consultation at a skilled nursing center. The patient was a 97 year old woman who was exhibiting symptoms of depression.

When I arrived at the facility I reviewed her chart and made my way to her room. There I found a very prim and proper lady sitting up in a chair and fully dressed. She invited me to have a seat, as she was expecting me, and knew the reason for my visit.

Following introductions, I began the process of getting to know her and assessing her symptoms. Her thinking was very clear, and she answered my questions readily.

After about fifteen minutes of conversation, she interrupted my interview abruptly by saying, "You can stop now."

I responded, "Stop what?"

She explained, "You can stop asking me questions. You see, I know you are trying to understand the reason for my depression, and I know very well why I'm depressed. I have been observing you as we've talked. I have decided that I can trust you, so I will tell you why I'm depressed and save us both some time."

Somewhat taken aback, I simply said, "OK, why are you depressed?"

She continued, "You see, I'm 97 years old. I know that, at best, I will only live two or three more years, but that isn't why I'm depressed. The reason that I'm depressed is that, when I look back over my life, I realize that I have lived my entire life for everyone else. I have spent my years trying to please everyone else or at least not displease them. I did what others wanted me to do. I lived my life for them while they were living their lives for themselves, and no one has lived a life for me, not even me. And now it's too late."

I was so struck with the lady's words that I have no idea what I said after that point. I hope I provided some comfort.

Applying the Parable

I have often thought of that lady and have been determined to live so that I will not echo her sorrows at the end of my life. I suggested that Andrew do the same.

Andrew's initial response was to grieve the time he had lost. He grieved the loss of Jennifer. He grieved the years he had spent pleasing others. His next response was anger. He was angry at his parents for controlling his life. He was angry at himself for not taking charge earlier and for being such a people pleaser.

Even though he recognized the changes he needed to make, making them wasn't so easy. He said that he wasn't even sure how to identify his wants and needs. I told him that he might want to start out by trying to identify small preferences or desires. We started with an exploration of possible activities he might enjoy. He made plans for dinner with a friend. He chose a movie he thought might be interesting. His goal was to make some choice every day that simply reflected a personal preference, a desire.

We then began working on more important choices. He decided to take an evening creative writing class. He didn't tell his parents until the class was well under way. He later brought in some of his writing, and I was truly impressed.

With time, Andrew learned to recognize his preferences. He gradually became more assertive with his parents and others in his life. He determined that he would not find himself regretting a life lived for others.

How much do you worry about others' opinions or work to try to please them? To what extent are your life choices guided by the potential approval or disapproval of those around you? Are you living your life for them while they are living their lives for themselves?

What are your dreams or desires? Do you even allow yourself to dream, and do you pursue those dreams? What do you want your life to look like? Is your life moving in that direction? Are you taking action to direct your life, or are you simply reacting? Are you living your life deliberately?

I'm not suggesting that you become self-centered or selfish. Time spent helping or doing for others is time well spent. I believe that we should love our neighbors, but I also believe that we should love ourselves. There should be a balance between taking care of other's needs and taking care of our own needs.

If you experienced events during childhood that wounded your self-esteem, you may have difficulty being assertive about your wants or needs. You may doubt your opinions or choices or you may be afraid of displeasing others. You may know what you want but have difficulty being assertive about it.

Proper assertiveness involves expressing your wants or needs in a balanced way. Consider the following scale:

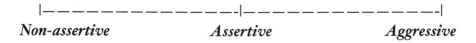

| Non-assertive | Assertive | Aggressive |

If you are non-assertive, you honor the other person's rights but don't honor your own rights. You comply with other's wishes and fail to express your own. If you are aggressive, you honor and defend your own rights, but do so in a manner that does not honor the other person's rights. You demand your way, while not considering the other person's needs or desires. If you are assertive, you honor and express your own desires and needs in a manner that also honors the rights of the other person.

Those with a wound of the heart tend to have difficulties with assertiveness. They often fluctuate between being non-assertive or aggressive. Most of the time, those with low self-esteem are non-assertive and they honor the needs of others but don't honor their own needs. Over time, they build up resentment that their needs are never met, and when that build-up reaches a certain level, they explode and express their needs in an aggressive way. Then there is a type of rebound reaction. They feel guilty for the aggression and go back to being non-assertive. They continue being non-assertive until the emotions once again build up, and they explode in an aggressive manner once again. As you can see, they skip assertiveness altogether. Being properly assertive allows you to avoid the difficulties inherent in non-assertiveness and aggression.

One way to determine whether a response is assertive is to imagine that your best friend gave that response under the exact circumstances you are experiencing. How would you feel about your friend's response? Would you feel that the response was appropriate? Would you feel that it was too aggressive? Would it simply be assertive? You would probably want your friend to give an assertive response and think that she had a right to do so.

The following exercises are designed to help you determine the extent to which you may have lived your life for others and to encourage you to listen to your preferences in the remainder of your life.

Write down any choices you made which were significantly determined by the opinions of others. These should be situations where you would have taken a different course if you had listened only to your opinion, wishes, or desires. If you had it to do over, would you have chosen differently? Can you change it now, or is it too late?

1. Life choices I made because of others' opinions or wishes:

----

2. Things I would like to do now but have hesitated because of someone's opinion:

----

3. Steps I can take to live my life deliberately:

----

4. List some life goals that come from your heart-goals that are independent of the good opinions of others.

    _____

    _____

    _____

    _____

    _____

    _____

    _____

5. Monitor your day-to-day behavior as to whether you are being non-assertive, aggressive, or assertive. Below write down any behaviors where you were:

Assertive:

    _____

    _____

    _____

    _____

    _____

    _____

    _____

Non-assertive:

    _____

    _____

    _____

    _____

    _____

    _____

    _____

Aggressive:

    _____

    _____

    _____

    _____

    _____

    _____

    _____

6. Reword any non-assertive or aggressive responses in a way that expresses the same feelings or desires in an assertive way.

_____

_____

_____

_____

_____

_____

_____

_____

Concluding Comments:

I've always said that most of what I know, I learned from my clients. This lady was certainly one of my teachers. A life spent in the service of others is a life well-spent, but a life which is dictated by the opinions of others is truly unfortunate.

Try to be conscious of the reasons behind your choices. My hope is that you will take care of others while still following your hopes and dreams. No one else can follow them for you.

Learning to be appropriately assertive is a lifelong task. Like everything else in this book, being assertive requires purpose, perception, and persistence. You have to have the intention to be assertive. You have to correctly perceive when an assertive response is needed and what one looks like. Finally, you have to be persistent in your attempts to be appropriately assertive.

The elderly lady taught me a great deal. If you listen to her, you will also learn the following:

1. Everyone is surrounded by people who have opinions, judgments, and preferences. Some of those people state their opinions strongly and loudly.

2. You also have your personal opinions and preferences for your life.

3. Like others, you have the right to express and pursue your preferences, wants and needs.

4. If you put too much emphasis on other's opinions or preferences, you will not follow your own desires, needs and wants.

5. If you ignore your desires long enough, you may actually lose touch with your preferences or wants.

6. Without change, you can find yourself having lived a life for others.

7. Don't wait until it's too late to live your life.

Chapter 14
Avoiding the Performance Trap

Being deeply loved by someone gives you strength, while loving someone deeply gives you courage.
Lao Tzu

Did you try to prove them wrong? Perhaps they said you would never succeed. Perhaps they called you stupid, loser or ignorant, or perhaps they suggested such things without ever saying those words. Perhaps they conveyed the message through other comments. "You'll never make it in college." "You can't do anything right." "What's wrong with you anyway?"

Some accept those messages as truth and choose a life of limits. They don't apply for college or the job promotion. They repeat the childhood messages throughout their lives, but they speak those messages in first person. "I'll never succeed." "I can't do anything right." "What's wrong with me?"

Others spend their lives trying to prove the messages to be wrong. They work hard. They push themselves. They succeed but never enough. Each success provides temporary relief from the nagging feelings of inadequacy. Such relief is short lived, however, as the old beliefs return as strong as ever. There seems to be an expectation that the next success, the next stellar performance will erase the memories of criticism or abuse. It doesn't work. It never does. No amount of success can repeal a childhood sentence of inadequacy.

It was his first session. As he entered my office, he tossed me a book. "This is why I'm here," he commented nonchalantly. The book was "The Impostor Phenomenon" by Pauline Clance. I knew this new client as Dr. Moore, but he asked me to call him Adam.

Adam had been practicing medicine in my community for over twenty years. He had an excellent reputation. He had previously taught at a medical hospital and had published several articles. Adam was active in the community and his church. He was a success by any standard.

Adam went on to tell me that he grew up "on the wrong side of the tracks." His parents were uneducated and poor. He noted that he made very good grades in school but wasn't accepted by his peers because of his family's poverty. Adam's self-esteem difficulties worsened at age 14 when he was sexually abused by a female neighbor. While looking at the floor, he commented that no one ever found out, but he knew all too well.

Adam said that everyone thought he was one person, but that he knew that he was actually someone else. He said he knew that he was really that kid from the other side of the tracks, the kid that didn't fit in, the kid that had sex with the woman next door. He believed that eventually everyone would find out who he really was, so he felt like an imposter.

All his life Adam had tried to achieve in an effort to prove that he wasn't really "that kid." He had worked all his life to disprove the messages from his childhood. The achievements came, but they disproved nothing. Nothing had changed inside.

In the meantime, Adam sacrificed a significant portion of his life pursuing the one achievement that would finally establish his worth. He had never married and had no children. He was alone, and he was lonely. All Adam's work, all his achievements, and all his success hadn't filled the empty place in his heart.

I told Adam that I had written a story to help children alter a performance-based self-esteem. I asked him if I could tell him a children's story and he agreed. I told him "The Parable of the Circus Horse." As you will see, this story also takes place in an old fashioned circus much like the one in the story of the helpless elephant.

The Parable of the
Circus Horse

☜☞

It was a land of dirt roads and poor farmers. Times were hard, and the routines of one day seemed to blend into the next. Thoughts of taking time for fun and excitement were rare.

But today was different. Today was fun. The circus was coming to town, and everyone seemed excited. This was one of those times when work could be set aside for fun.

This was an old fashioned circus with wooden wagons carrying wild animals, a little brass band and one large tent. There were, of course, clowns and acrobats; but the star of this circus was a large, beautiful, white performing horse.

This circus horse could do many tricks. She pranced with her head and tail held high. The children laughed, the ladies cheered, and the gentlemen smiled each time she performed her act.

The horse loved to hear the applause from the crowd. She worked very hard to make sure she did her tricks perfectly. She worked hard because the applause felt good. The horse loved the attention of the crowd when she performed, but something was missing. This horse knew that something was missing.

After each performance, her trainer would lead her back to her dark stable to wait for the next show. She would wait there alone, remembering the sound of the cheers and applause. Remembering it made her feel good, but something was missing.

One day during a performance a little boy was playing with matches behind the circus tent. He accidently caught the tent on fire. Dry canvas burns very quickly and the fire spread. People were running in all directions to escape. The animals broke loose and ran as well.

The circus horse ran away as fast as she could. She ran, terrified, into some woods beside the tent. She ran and she ran. As she ran, she bumped into trees and ran through bushes and briars. She fell down in the mud.

By the time she stopped running, she was muddy and tired. Briars and sticks were stuck in her mane and tail. She wasn't holding her head and tail high at all now, but worst of all, she was lost. She had no idea how to get out of the woods.

After wandering in the forest for several days, she came upon a clearing. At the edge of the clearing, she could see a farm in the distance. There was a fenced pasture that came almost to the edge of the forest. On the other side of the pasture, she could see a house and a barn.

Tired and hungry, the horse stood there looking at the farm for a long time. Then a little boy from the farm saw her. He ran across the pasture to get a better look. He ran all the way to the fence, calling out to her. The little boy stopped at the fence because his parents wouldn't let him go any further. Leaning over the fence, he called out to her again.

The circus horse kept her distance and just watched him. She was afraid. As the sun went down, the little boy had to go back to his house; but she didn't leave. She waited in the clearing through the night.

The next morning the little boy came running across the pasture again to see her. This time he carried a bag of apples. He leaned over the fence holding out an apple and calling out to her. The horse watched but kept her distance. She was hungry, but she was afraid.

The little boy didn't give up. He kept calling her and holding out the apple. After a while, the horse moved a little bit closer, then a little bit closer. Finally, she was close enough for him to feed her the apple. She was so hungry.

As the horse ate the apple, the boy rubbed her nose and put his arm around her neck. It felt good. Then suddenly she knew.

This was what had been missing! She was muddy and dirty. She wasn't beautiful now. She wasn't performing now. Her head and tail were hanging down, and he loved her anyway. This was so much better than performing. This was so much better than applause. This was what she had been missing all along!

From that day forth, the horse lived on the farm with the little boy. He loved her just for who she was. She loved him back, and nothing was missing any more.

Applying the Parable

I wrote this story in an attempt to address the tendency many have to base their perceived value on their performance. Many people have a performance-based self-esteem, where their perceived worth rises and falls with each success or failure.

When a child experiences criticism, he will often develop a performance-based self-esteem. His wound of the heart is inadequacy, so he either works very hard to succeed, in hopes of healing the wound, or he resigns himself to feeling inadequate. Either course is doomed to failure; however, as each failure worsens the feelings of inadequacy, and no amount of success can heal such a wound.

Each unsuccessful performance takes on a new importance, and failure becomes an unacceptable option. I often share the following example, provided by Denis Waitley, Ph.D., a motivational psychologist.

Imagine that I placed a twenty foot long board on the ground. The board was four inches thick and twelve inches wide. I asked you to walk across the board from one end to the other, without stepping off. I offered you $100.00 if you could do it without falling off. Would you try? Of course you would- easy task, sufficient reward, but now imagine that I took that same board and put one end on the roof of a four story building. I put the other end on the roof of an adjacent four story building such that there was a four story alley below the board. I asked you to do the same task of walking across from one end to the other without stepping off. Would you do it for $100.00? How about for $200.00?

Why not? What's the difference? The difference is the penalty for failure. If you step off in the first situation, you simply lose the money. If you step off in the second situation, you lose your life.

Many people see every situation as if the board were on the four story building when, actually, it is on the ground. They view every performance as if the consequence were life or death. And in a sense, it is, if they feel it will be the life or death of their self-esteem.

The only real healing for an inadequacy heart wound is found within. The person has to recognize that his actual value is inherent in who he is, not in what he does. Feeling valued, even when failing or when not performing at all, can aid in the healing process.

Trying to prove your worth or competency by pursuing achievement is like trying to fill a bucket with a hole in the bottom. It won't stay full, regardless of the amount of water you pour into it. No amount of achievement will ever be enough.

Adam admitted that his fear of failing was enormous. He said he knew better, but every performance felt like life-or-death.

As the story suggests, the recognition earned by achievement is a poor substitute for unconditional love. Having someone love us when we are not performing, when we are dirty and down, can be a powerful boost to a wounded heart. The realization that we can be valued and accepted, even when we are vulnerable, can be enormously healing.

That is, of course, if we accept the love. Unfortunately, we often have a difficulty accepting unconditional love when we have a wound of the heart. It doesn't feel right. We don't feel we deserve it. We feel that we must earn the right to be valued.

In fact, when unconditional love is offered to a person with a heart wound, that person tends to devalue the one offering the love. I use the following example to illustrate this principle to my clients.

Imagine that you have a car for sale. You put a "For Sale" sign in the windshield and park it in your yard beside the road. One day, a man stops and says he's interested in your car. He checks it out, test drives it, and says he wants to make you an offer. He says that he hates to haggle over price, so he's just going to make one offer. If that amount is sufficient, he will buy the car. If not, he will go on his way with no hard feelings.

You haven't told him what you're asking for the car. It's an older car with some dings in the paint and some tears in the upholstery. You figured you might be able to get $1000 for it. You had planned on asking $2000 to give yourself some negotiating room.

He looks at the car again and presents his offer. "I can't pay you a penny more than $10,000 for it." You try to keep a straight face and reply, "I suppose I can sell it for $10,000." Remember, you had been willing to take $1000.

The man writes you a check. It clears the bank. You transfer the title. It's all good.

My question for you is this. What's your opinion of the man? Usual responses are, "He's an idiot" or "He has more money than he has sense."

Two weeks later, you see a picture of this man in your local paper. He's standing in front of your car. The caption under the picture reads that he just came back from a national auto show. The car was one of a series that was discontinued after only twenty were manufactured. It says the car is actually worth about $25,000. The man doesn't seem so foolish now.

The point of the story is this. You had something you thought was just worth $1000. This man came along and said it was worth $10,000. You didn't change your opinion of the value of the car. You changed your opinion of the value of the man.

If you sustained a wound of the heart, you probably think of yourself as a $1000 car, complete with dings and upholstery tears. If someone comes along and says that you are actually a $10,000 car, you will hold onto your estimation of your value while devaluing the other person, feeling that something must be wrong with him.

I gave Adam some homework to help him examine the role of success and failure in his life. That homework was as follows:

1. Think about the degree to which your self-esteem rests on your ability to perform or succeed. One way to examine this is to reflect on your response to failure. No one likes to fail, but some people allow failure to crush them. Their feelings of worth plummet when they are confronted with any failure. There is a major difference between wanting to succeed and feeling you must succeed. Think about any recent performance situations. How did you feel as you were approaching the situation? How would you have reacted to failure? List some performance situations below.

————————————————————————————————

————————————————————————————————

————————————————————————————————

————————————————————————————————

----

2. Try to imagine how those performance situations would
    have been different if you simply wanted to do your best
    but didn't feel your worth was riding on success. Could
    you lessen your fears of failure? Would you have enjoyed
    the experience more? Would you have been more com-
    fortable? Finally, would you have been more successful
    without the fears of failure?

    ----

3. This week try to identify those people in your life who love
    you without your having to perform-those who already
    give you unconditional love. If you don't have such persons
    in your life now, try to imagine what it would look like if
    you were able to give yourself unconditional love. Think
    about how you might value yourself even when you are not
    performing. Write down your thoughts below.

    ----

4. Examine your attitude when you face performance situations. Are you viewing the task as if the board is on the building or on the ground? See if you can remind yourself that most tasks are not life or death. Remind yourself that your worth is based on who you are and not what you do.

Concluding Comments:

It's difficult to recognize when a wounded heart expresses itself as a drive to perform. The victims look so successful and competent. We tend to assume that they have it all together. We can even be intimidated by them. Most would never guess that, behind that successful façade, they harbor feelings of inadequacy and rejection. Like the circus horse, however, they know that, after the performance, they are left with the feeling that something is missing.

Many "successful" people live their lives with the vague feeling that something is missing. Unfortunately, they tend to look to the next challenge and accomplishment, in hopes that they will discover that something. It never works.

The only solution for a wounded heart is the hard work of healing that wound. Examining and changing one's beliefs about oneself can produce such healing. Only then, can the person pursue a challenge as something he wants, but not something he needs to prove his value.

Through tragedy, the circus horse discovered what was missing in her life. In the process of doing so, she conveyed some powerful truths. These are as follows:

1. We can sometimes get caught up in the belief that we have to prove our worth by performance or achievement.

2. No amount of success or achievement can fully meet our emotional needs.

3. We all need to feel that we are loved and valued unconditionally.

4. We need to know that we have value, even when we are bruised, down, and dirty.

5.   When we recognize our true worth we are able to enjoy our performances and pursuits without overwhelming fears of failure.
6.   Most of our life tasks are like the board on the ground, not like the board high up on the building.

Denis Waitley, Ph.D., "The Psychology of Winning," Berkley Press, 1986.

Chapter 15
The Impact of Sexual Abuse

Child abuse casts a shadow the length of a lifetime.
Herbert Ward

The deepest wound of the heart occurs when the child is abused. Abuse can be physical, emotional or sexual, a one-time event or a repeated occurrence over several years. I have worked with many abused children and many adults who were abused as children. The wounds are deep and enduring.

I fully believe and often say to the abuse survivor that those who are abused as children are totally innocent victims. The child can do nothing to prompt, invite or cause an adult to abuse her. The child is also helpless to prevent the adult from abusing her.

When an adult survivor of abuse considers other abused children, she knows those children are helpless and innocent. She recognizes that all the blame for the abuse rests on the shoulders of the abuser, not the child. She recognizes that there is never an excuse for abuse, but when the abuse survivor considers her own abuse, she recognizes none of that.

Any form of abuse can be devastating to the victim, but sexual abuse creates a unique wound of the heart. All too frequently, I have seen the severe impact of sexual abuse on my patients' self-esteem. While all the principles outlined in this book apply to the wound created by sexual abuse, the particular characteristics of such wounds warrant special attention.

There are four common, almost universal, beliefs held by sexual abuse victims. These beliefs seem to prevail, regardless of the age when the abuse occurred. It doesn't seem to matter whether the child was three or thirteen. These beliefs are often even expressed by adults who are sexually assaulted or raped. It also doesn't seem to matter whether the sexual abuse was a one-time occurrence or repeated assaults over a period of years. The effect appears to be the same whether the perpetrator was a stranger, an acquaintance or a family member. The particular circumstances of the abuse do not seem to alter the resulting beliefs. These common beliefs are as follows:

1. There was something about me that made the abuser choose me. I must have done or said something wrong to cause the abuse to occur. I'm bad.

2. Now that I have been abused, I am defective, dirty, and damaged. Others wouldn't want to spend time with me if they knew what I had done. They wouldn't like me or love me. I'm bad.

3. I should have been able to stop the abuse or stop it earlier than I did. I should have done something to make it stop. I'm bad. (Interestingly, this belief is held, even when the victim was five years old or younger and the perpetrator was an adult.)

4. The victim perceives her sexuality differently. She may gravitate toward sex, even when she would rather say no. The victim will often feel that sex is the only thing that anyone would want from her, or that she might as well give in because she is already broken. Because of her increased sexual activity, she concludes, "I'm bad." On the other hand, the victim may experience anxiety or repulsion in association with sex. She may not enjoy sex or avoid it altogether, even when it occurs in acceptable circumstances.

These beliefs are deeply engrained and difficult to change. Much of my work with abuse victims involves changing these beliefs.

There is another common reaction to sexual abuse that is rarely discussed, yet it can be the greatest contributor to the victim's feelings of shame and self-blame. This is the occurrence of physical or sexual arousal during the abuse.

The human body has many automatic responses. Certain types of stimulation can trigger sexual arousal, even if the stimulation is totally unwanted and unwelcomed. Such arousal can best be compared to the knee jerk reflex when a doctor taps the knee with a rubber hammer. If the patient's reflexes are normal, a tap on a specific part of the knee will elicit an upward jerk of the leg. It is involuntary, and you can't prevent it, regardless of how hard you might try.

An arousal response during sexual abuse simply reflects an automatic reflex in the body and does not mean that the victim asked for, enjoyed, or wanted the abuse. It does not change the fact that the victim was innocent of blame.

Yet many victims misinterpret such arousal to mean that they must have wanted the abuse or been a cooperating party in the action. This is not true. I have heard victims say, "My body betrayed me," when discussing this issue. That's not true. Your body simply reacted in a normal human way.

Another common concern of victims relates to their cognitive experience during abuse. Many times they report that their minds seemed to "check out" when the abuse was occurring. They indicated that they felt as if they were watching the event from a distance or that their minds became numb. They said that everything "felt unreal." This is normal. It is the brain's way of helping the victim survive the experience, nothing more. It seems that "the head checks out and the body checks in" during sexual abuse. This is a normal reaction to an abnormal event.

Unfortunately, I have had much experience counseling victims of sexual abuse, too much. The stories are too similar, the pain too deep, the experience too common. Sandra told one of those stories.

She hadn't come in for counseling because of the sexual abuse. They rarely do. She came in because of depression. During the assessment, she revealed a strong tendency to be self-critical. She later shared that her low self-esteem was, in-part, the result of sexual abuse.

Sandra reported that she was first abused by her grandfather at age four. He served as her babysitter until she started school. He sexually abused her almost every day that he "took care of her." It didn't end until she started school. He told her that her parents would send her away if she told, and she believed him.

When Sandra was thirteen, the grandfather was accused of molesting a girl from the neighborhood. Several family members commented that he had always seemed like "a dirty old man." Her report of her abuse began with, "Then, why did you have him babysit me?"

She told me that by the time she was thirteen she had also been abused by an uncle and a neighbor. These were one-time occurrences, but they sufficiently deepened the wound of the heart inflicted by the grandfather. The experience with three different perpetrators convinced Sandra that there was something about her that invited the abuse.

Sandra had all the typical reactions to sexual abuse previously listed. When she did reveal the abuse to her family at age thirteen, they scolded her for not telling them earlier. They then cautioned her to never tell anyone else. This deepened her sense of shame. Sandra said her abuse was never mentioned again, but she felt the family treated her differently after that. Because of her family's reaction, she didn't bother to tell them about the later abuse incidents at all.

When she learned about her grandfather's abuse of another child, thirteen-year-old Sandra chastised herself for not having told someone earlier. Perhaps, she noted, she could have prevented him from abusing the neighborhood girl and who knows how many others.

After age thirteen Sandra didn't speak of the abuse. She said she had not even told her husband for fear that he would see her differently. Her secret wounded the marriage relationship in subtle ways.

Sandra reported that her adolescent and young adult years were fairly promiscuous. She often said "yes" to sex when she wanted to say no. Sandra lamented that she was afraid she would be rejected if she refused since she believed that sex was all she had to offer a man. I told Sandra that her reactions were very normal and that she was, in fact, a totally innocent victim. I told her "The Parable of the Totally Innocent Victim," to illustrate the concept.

The Parable of the
Totally Innocent Victim

৵৹৽

I turned the TV on that morning to find one of those Special News Reports. The camera crews were already on the scene. A passenger jet had taken off from the airport in Washington, DC in the early morning hours of January 13, 1982. The wings had not been completely de-iced, so an ice coating remained. Because of the ice, the plane was too heavy and began an uncontrolled descent, after only rising a few hundred feet.

As the plane fell to the earth, it crashed through the 14th Street Bridge which spanned the Potomac River. The plane landed in the river. When I tuned in, I saw this large passenger jet lying half submerged in the river. Spotlights were illuminating the scene as rescue crews worked to get the surviving passengers out of the plane and to the shore.

I watched silently as the rescuers pulled one victim after another out of the plane, some alive and some dead. I watched with the rest of the world to see if the bodies were moving or lifeless.

As I later thought about the accident, I realized that there were three categories of victims involved but that only one group of victims was totally innocent. The first group of victims consisted of members of the crew. Some of them were killed in the crash. They were victims, but they weren't totally innocent because they worked for the airline. They shared the airline's responsibility to make sure the plane was ready for take off, even if only by association.

The second group of victims consisted of passengers on the plane. Some of them were also killed. They were relatively innocent of responsibility. After all, they assumed the airline took the necessary steps to insure that the plane was ready for take-off, but they weren't totally innocent victims since they had purchased a ticket and boarded the plane. We buy a plane ticket, knowing that sometimes planes do crash. We choose to fly knowing the inherent risks.

The third group of victims was "totally innocent." Can you guess who they were? They were the commuters driving across the bridge. They had no association with the airline. They hadn't chosen to fly that day. They were just driving to work as they had every other day. They just happened to be at the wrong place at the wrong time. If these victims had been thirty seconds earlier or thirty seconds later in crossing the bridge, they would have been spared.

Isn't that also the case with children who are abused? They don't do anything to bring about the abuse. They are helpless to stop the abuse. They are simply in the wrong place at the wrong time with the wrong person, and they are there through no fault of their own.

Knowing that you were totally innocent doesn't take away the pain of the experience, but it can take away the secondary and sometimes deeper pain of blaming yourself. My goal in working with an abuse victim is to help them eliminate that secondary pain of self-blame to help them realize that they were "totally innocent victims."

Applying the Parable

Sandra was able to intellectually agree that any victim of sexual abuse is totally innocent, even her. She didn't emotionally connect to this fact until I asked her to imagine that she found out today that her daughter had been abused. I asked her to imagine that the daughter experienced the same abusive acts that she had experienced so many years ago. Her body stiffened. Her face revealed her anger.

I asked Sandra if she would blame her daughter for the abuse, and she exclaimed somewhat indignantly, "Of course not. It wouldn't be her fault." She paused and stared at me. I reminded her that she was not at fault either. During the rest of the session, we worked through the differences in Sandra's perceptions of her abuse and the perceptions she would have if the victim were her daughter.

Of course, it took several sessions for Sandra to shift her realization of her innocence from her head to her heart. She said several times that she just felt that she was somehow different. Her mind seemed intent on finding a way to place some blame on that little girl that she used to be. As I said earlier, the human mind has a strong tendency to hold on to existing beliefs, even when those beliefs are false and self-destructive.

Over time, Sandra gradually accepted that her abuse was not her fault. Once she accepted this truth fully, she felt compassion for that child she used to be. As she did so, her depression improved significantly.

I had a check-up session with Sandra about a year later. She said she hadn't told anyone that she was abused, but that she had been approached by three different female acquaintances who said they needed to talk to her about something very personal. They then proceeded to tell her about their own sexual abuse experience. They said they had the feeling that she would be helpful. This connection amazed Sandra since they hadn't previously known about her abuse. Following their revelation, Sandra shared her story and offered support. She said that she even had them imagine their reactions if their abuse had been visited upon another child.

Sandra said that she felt good that her painful experiences had proven to be of help to other victims. She related that each time she told another woman that the abuse wasn't her fault, she reminded herself of the same truth, the truth that she and they were totally innocent victims.

Today would be a good time for you to begin the process of recognizing that you were an innocent victim of your abuse. It happened to you, but there was nothing about you that triggered it. It hurt you, but it didn't lesson your value in any way. You couldn't stop it, but that didn't mean you were at fault or weak. There were many reasons why you were powerless to stop it. If you could have, you would have. It did impact your perceptions of your own sexuality and your subsequent sexual choices, but that was a normal response to a very abnormal event. The exercises below should help bring these truths home for you.

Imagine that a good friend called you today and asked you to meet her for lunch. She sounded troubled and said she needed someone to talk to. After settling in for lunch, your friend began her story. She said that some recent events had brought back terrible memories from childhood, and she needed to talk about them. She indicated that she had never told another soul. She then related that she was sexually abused as a child. Imagine that your abuse hadn't happened to you but instead had happened to her. She experienced exactly the same abuse that you experienced. Now imagine you are listening to her story. What would your response be? How would you feel about her? Write your response to your friend as if you are talking to her.

1. What would you say to your friend? Write some statements down below.

_____

_____

_____

_____

_____

_____

_____

_____

_____

_____

2. Now, imagine that you are speaking to that child you used to be at the age of your abuse. What words do you say to that little girl you used to be?

_____

_____

_____

_____

_____

_____

_____

_____

_____

_____

_____

3. Did you show the same compassion and support for yourself that you showed for your friend?

4. Think about the differences between your response to your friend's story of her abuse and the way you think about your own abuse. How much more compassionate were you to your friend than you usually are to yourself? Most people tend to make more reassuring statements to a friend while making more cautionary or "you should have" statements to themselves. Refer to your response to your friend and write below a similarly compassionate response to yourself?

_____

_____

_____

_____

_____

_____

_____

_____

_____

_____

_____

_____

_____

_____

5. If possible, look at a photograph of yourself at the age of your abuse. Notice how small and helpless the little girl or boy in the photo is. Also, think about a child you currently know who is about the same age. Notice how small and helpless that child is. Imagine that child experiencing the same abuse. Then, remember the age and power of the abuser. Remind yourself of the following truths:

a. That little child who used to be you couldn't have done anything to initiate the abuse. She was just a normal little girl. The abuser was totally responsible.

b. That child was hurt by the abuse, but she was and is as good as any other little child. She was still precious. She was no less valuable.

c. That child did not have the power to stop the abuse. She was helpless. She was afraid. She was overwhelmed.

d. The mistakes you later made regarding sex were the direct result of the sexual abuse you experienced.

6. If you have trouble applying those statements to yourself, imagine applying them to your friend. Would these reassurances come more easily if you were speaking them to a friend?

7. Imagine if your own child experienced the abuse. Imagine that you found out today that your child was abused in exactly the same way you were abused. Would you be angry? How angry would you be? How angry would you be at your child? What? So, you wouldn't be angry at your child? Why not? Your response might be, "Because it wasn't her fault." Doesn't that also apply to that child that used to be you? Could you apply the statements to that child from years past?

Concluding Comments:

At the beginning of this chapter, I stated that sexual abuse creates a unique wound of the heart. The pattern of negative self-beliefs outlined in this chapter is almost universal. The wound is certainly deep and painful, and the impact of the wound is seen in every aspect of the victim's life.

The child's tendency toward self-blame for the abuse seems to inflict the most damage. That self-blame creates a lingering sense of shame, and shame always cuts deeply into the victim's heart.

Only when the individual fully recognizes that she was a totally innocent victim, can true healing begin. She begins to see herself without the secret shadow of guilt and shame.

The unfortunate victims driving across the Potomac on the 14th Street Bridge have illustrated some important truths. These are:

1. Sometimes horrible things happen to us, even when we did absolutely nothing to deserve or cause them.

2. We can be hurt simply because we are in the wrong place at the wrong time.

3. Sexual abuse victims are "totally innocent victims" who are simply in the wrong place, at the wrong time, with the wrong person.

4. Sexual abuse is always the fault of the perpetrator or abuser.

5. All sexual abuse victims are left with a deep feeling that the abuse was somehow their fault or that they did something wrong. This feeling is always inaccurate and devastating.

Chapter 16
You Can't Love People Enough to Change Them

Consider how hard it is to change yourself and you will realize how little chance you have in trying to change others. Benjamin Franklin

Our culture has many myths regarding relationships. The typical fairy tale ends with "And they lived happily ever after." We see in the movies that the bad man changed for the love of a good woman. We persist in the belief that we can change another person if we can just find the right behavior, if we can find the right key.

The spouse or child of the alcoholic, the drug user, or the batterer searches for something he can do that will stop the painful behavior. "Don't make him mad." "I shouldn't have fussed." "I don't care if she was wrong. Go apologize and she'll calm down." "Be good now so daddy won't be stressed and start drinking again."

I think the tendency to personalize blame begins in childhood. Children are egocentric so they assume blame for everything. When their parents divorce, they feel they did something wrong. When a parent is critical they believe they were inadequate. When a parent is uninvolved they believe they were unlovable.

The tendency to believe we have the power to change others begins early. It provides the basis for codependency, a pattern of behaviors first described in substance abuse treatment. The codependent person's sense of worth becomes dependent on the behaviors of the addict. When the addict is doing well the codependent spouse feels loved or worthwhile. When the addict is doing poorly the spouse feels unloved, worthless, or that he or she has failed.

The tendency isn't limited to the family of an abuser. The husband of the critical wife believes that she would be accepting of him if he could just do the right thing to please her. The wife of the adulterous husband wonders what the other woman has that she doesn't have. What's wrong with her that made him do it?

The behaviors may differ, but the pattern is the same. "If I can just do or say the right things they will be good to me." Some search their entire lives in vain.

I once heard a psychologist say that people can be divided into two personality types: onion people and garlic people. He said onion people are like an onion. If you eat an onion, it can have a strong taste. It can cause heartburn and indigestion. It can cause discomfort or pain to the one eating it, but onion breath isn't too bad. If you eat garlic, it doesn't have a strong taste. It doesn't usually cause heartburn or indigestion. Garlic causes no discomfort or pain to the one eating it, but garlic breath reeks.

The psychologist said that onion people tend to be very hard on themselves. Onion people cause pain to themselves, but they work very hard to avoid hurting anyone else. On the other hand, garlic people are never hard on themselves. Garlic people cause no pain for themselves, but they hurt everyone around them. They take no blame but are quick to place the blame on others. You can usually identify those people in your life that are onion people and those that are garlic people.

We have to respond to onion people and garlic people differently. The nicer you are to an onion person, the nicer they will be to you. If you are kind to them, they will usually respond with kindness.

You can't deal with a garlic person in the same way. A garlic person treats people with respect if they stand up to them. They treat a person well only when they sense the person will put up with nothing less. When a garlic person encounters people who have trouble standing up for themselves, they will crush them. They show no respect for them. The harder one tries to please a garlic person, the worse the garlic person treats him.

I once worked with a couple, Pete and Melinda, who exemplified the concept of an onion person with a garlic person. In the beginning, she seemed to think he was wonderful. He said they dated for two years and rarely had an argument. All that seemed to change after the marriage.

Pete said that he never seemed to please his wife, Melinda. At first she was simply critical of his chores around the house. She wanted the grass cut in a certain pattern and he never seemed to get it right. She said he didn't know how to fold clothes and couldn't clean adequately. He tried to listen to her directives and do better but never did.

After a time, she began to complain about their house being small and their never having enough money. She compared him to other men in their circle of friends and pointed out how they provided better than he. She even called him a loser and a failure at times.

Then Melinda's criticism migrated to the bedroom. She complained about his lack of skills at lovemaking, even saying at times that he wasn't much of a man.

Pete was in an emotional trap. He had believed himself to be inadequate long before he married Melinda, and her verbal abuse simply worsened the wound. His response to each criticism was to try harder. He said he came in to see me to find out what was wrong with him. He wanted me to tell him how he could improve so that she would be pleased with him.

I told him that I couldn't do that. I told him that Melinda's criticism was a problem within her and not the result of his inadequacy. I told him that I would help him learn to be assertive with her and that I would work with both if she wanted to accompany him to a session. I told Pete that his situation reminded me of "The Parable of the Old Man and the Rattlesnake."

The Parable of the
Old Man and the Rattlesnake

స్ళం

Even in early October, the days can be very cold in the desert. This day was colder than most. The north wind blew in bone chilling gusts. The sun was beginning to set, but it was hard to tell since the sky was overcast.

The old man was a loner, but today he was feeling especially lonely. Loneliness was an unusual feeling for him, and it felt strange in his gut. He didn't trust people but didn't have to worry about it much as he had arranged his life to see as little of them as possible.

He had about a half mile more to walk before he reached his home, such as it was. He lived in a small cabin he had built himself out in the desert. It was far enough from people that most left him alone. This arrangement usually suited him fine; but today for some reason he felt the cold of isolation along with the cold of the coming winter.

As he walked along the dirt path, his feet tended to shuffle, stirring up small dust clouds with each step. He wrapped his coat tighter around his belly as he cursed the cold. He was only half paying attention but he noticed the thing on the side of the road.

It was lying in the clumps of grass and blended in with the dirt and rocks quite well. The man, now curious, walked over to get a closer look. Sure enough it was what he had suspected. It was a medium sized rattlesnake lying there as pretty as you please.

Now the man knew that you don't usually see rattlesnakes lying out in the cold like that. By this time they should be safely hidden in their dens for the winter. Left out in the cold, they will slowly freeze to death. This one was almost there. It was still alive but barely so. The man knew that the thing would never survive the night.

Right now he was satisfied with just studying the creature. He admired its markings and gazed as its muscles very slowly contracted. It was trying to move enough to get back to the relative warmth of its den, but the effort was futile.

As the old man watched the slow life-and-death drama, he had a strange thought. He envisioned the idea of a guard rattlesnake. That's right-a guard rattlesnake. What if he could save its life? What if he could take care of it? It would be loyal to him. It would protect him much like a loyal guard dog.

Without much more thought than that, the man picked the snake up and put it in his coat pocket. He could feel the cold in its stiff body as he slid it down into the coat and made his way home.

When he reached his house, the creature was still stiff and barely breathing. The old man had been thinking about his life-saving plan all the way home. He placed the snake on a soft warm pillow he had laid on the hearth. He then covered its body except for the head with an old army blanket. The old man built up the fire in the fireplace and put a dish of water in front of its head. He did everything he could think of to make the creature comfortable and bring it back to life.

The old man sat down on the floor beside the creature and gently rubbed its head. He wanted to be the first thing it saw when it came back to life. He wanted it to have no doubt that he was the one that saved its life. The old man wanted the snake to appreciate him and to be loyal to him. To even his surprise, he had the thought that he wanted the snake to love him.

The fire began to burn more brightly. The room warmed slowly. The old man, now sitting very still, began to drift off to sleep.

They say that the bite of a rattlesnake brings an intense pain. It was definitely enough to waken the old man with a start. The prick of the fangs was nothing compared to the feeling of the venom shooting up his arm. As he jerked his arm back, the snake let go, but it was too late. The damage was done.

As the old man lay there dying, he turned to the rattlesnake and asked, "Why did you do this to me? I did everything for you! You were dying when I found you! I saved your life. I got you water and warmth. Why did you do this?"

The snake cocked his head slightly as he hissed, "I'm a rattlesnake. That's what we do."

Applying the Parable

People generally behave in a way that is consistent with who they are. If you enter into a relationship with a rattlesnake, you should expect to get bitten. That's just what they do. Sometimes we believe that we can change other people if we just love them enough. It doesn't work. It never works. We can't change others. Sometimes people do change, but they change because they want to change, not because someone else changes them.

When someone is emotionally abusive to us, it is important for us to recognize that those behaviors are simply characteristic of that person. When your self-esteem is already wounded, your tendency is to assume that they treat you badly because there is something wrong with you.

There was nothing the man could have done to make the snake love him. The snake did what was typical of him. He bit and pumped venom into the first body part he could reach. He did what rattlesnakes do.

There was nothing you could have done to make the abusive person love you. They couldn't show you love because they didn't know how. They were abusive because that is who they are. They did what was typical of them.

Recognizing that you didn't deserve the abuse doesn't remove the hurt completely. You still bruise if they hit you, pinch you, or worse and it still hurts if they call you names or put you down. Recognizing that you didn't deserve the abuse keeps it from damaging your self-esteem further.

Another person may be abusive to us only once, but when we believe the abusive lies and repeat them in our thoughts, we continue the abuse for the rest of our lives. We become the abuser as well as the victim.

It took several sessions before Pete said he was ready to be assertive with Melinda. Confrontations made him very anxious, but he knew it had to be done. At my suggestion, he wrote his thoughts in a letter first. He sat down with her as she read the letter. They then talked for about an hour. He told her that her criticism wasn't fair and how it made him feel.

At first Melinda reacted as Pete would predict. She became very angry. Normally Pete would have backed down; but he stayed in the moment and remained assertive. That first conversation ended with her saying that he could leave if he wasn't satisfied with her. He let her know that he had no intention of leaving, but that he didn't deserve her criticism.

Melinda's behaviors didn't change at first. Pete had to be assertive with her each time she treated him badly. Over the next few weeks, Melinda did change her behaviors toward Pete. As she gradually recognized that he would not tolerate her verbal abuse, her criticism calmed down; and she actually gave him some compliments. The relationship gradually became more equal.

Sometimes the person doesn't change. Sometimes with all our efforts and assertiveness, the abuser continues to abuse. Sometimes we simply have to get away from the abuser to protect ourselves.

Here are some of the homework exercises that I gave Pete to help him deal with Melinda's behaviors. If this story makes you think of someone in your life, complete the following:

1. Make a list of the negative behaviors you have experienced or observed in that person. This would include actions, statements, and looks.

Negative Behaviors exhibited by: _____

1. _____
2. _____
3. _____
4. _____
5. _____
6. _____
7. _____
8. _____
9. _____
10. _____
11. _____

12. _____

13. _____

14. _____

15. _____

2. Now, take those behaviors you listed above and label them: "_____isms." Put the person's first name in the blank. For example, a Phillipism is a behavior that is typical of Phillip. A Maryism is a behavior that is typical of someone named Mary.

3. If those behaviors are typical of the person, they are not caused by you. Remember, people usually act like themselves.

4. Once you realize that the hurtful person's negative behaviors are not caused by your inadequacies, you begin to see the need to be assertive. When you are assertive with them, you establish boundaries for the behaviors you can tolerate in the relationship. Below, write down some assertive statements you need to say to your hurtful person.

Assertive Statements:

1. _____

2. _____

3. _____

4. _____

5. _____

6. _____

Concluding Comments:

There's something about a wound of the heart that causes the victim to fall into a trap. I don't fully understand why, but I see it happening all the time. The traps are different but the effect is the same.

In Chapter 12, we discussed the trap of helplessness. When the wounded one perceives herself to be helpless, she doesn't take action to change her life. Her life then stays the same, reinforcing that belief that she is helpless.

In Chapter 13, we discussed the trap of performance. When the wounded one perceives that he must perform or achieve to attain worth, he structures his life around achievement. The achievement never fulfills his need for worth, and his performance focus decreases his chances of finding the love he longs for in a healthy relationship.

In this chapter, we discussed the trap of co-dependency. Here, the wounded one perceives that she can prove her worth and competency by changing another person. She believes that she can make an unloving person love her, a bad person be good, or an unhappy person be happy, if she can just find the right key or do the right thing. Since it is impossible to change another human being, she is doomed to failure, thus reinforcing her belief that she is incompetent and worthless.

The old man and the rattlesnake illustrated some important truths about relationships. These are:

1. We sometimes falsely believe that we can change people if we love them enough or if we can please them enough.

2. People usually behave in a manner that is characteristic of themselves.

3. People who are hurtful will hurt us if we get close enough to them.

4. The only way to deal with a hurtful person is to establish boundaries by being assertive or by distancing ourselves from them.

5. A one-time act of assertiveness won't be enough. We must be persistently assertive whenever the person treats us badly.

6. The hurtful person has to know that we will no longer put up with her treating us badly.

7. Even then she may not change, and we may have to back away from her to protect ourselves.

"The Parable of the Old Man and the Rattlesnake" was inspired by the Cherokee legend, "The Little Boy and the Rattlesnake."

Chapter 17
Putting It All Together

I realize that the mission of this book is enormous. Nonetheless, the tools contained herein can give you a new perspective of yourself. If you took the time to consider the message of each chapter and completed the homework exercises, you should be on your way to that goal.

That said, you are just at the beginning of the work. Core beliefs are well-engrained and difficult to change. Those old thought patterns have become as natural to you as breathing. They are woven into the fabric of your life. You chip away one day at a time. Some days you realize the benefits of a healthy self-esteem, and other days you feel as if you are back at square one.

The last of the three principles of Purpose, Perception, and Persistence is Persistence for a reason. From this point forward, your progress will depend on your persistence. You will, in fact, need to continue challenging your negative core beliefs for the rest of your life; but the work should gradually get much easier.

Sometimes the work will focus on cultivating an attitude of compassion for that child you used to be or for yourself in the present. To do this, you may need to go back and review one of the stories, like "The Time Machine" or "The Violin Nobody Wanted" or those entire chapters. The work may involve asking yourself whether you are being the Good Coach or the Bad Coach to yourself and trying to respond to your mistake as the Good Coach would. Sometimes your compassion toward your inner child will be helped by sitting quietly and meditating on a childhood picture of yourself, remembering how young, innocent and helpless that child was. You may need to write a new letter to that little girl or boy to clarify your feelings.

In some situations the work will focus on correcting inaccurate perceptions of current circumstances which have been distorted by your wound of the heart. Of course, you must first hold an awareness of the type of perceptual errors your heart wound creates. Does your wound cause you to inaccurately perceive rejection, or does it cause you to inaccurately perceive failure, judgment, or criticism? Which direction is your mirror curved?

To do this work of perceptual change, you will need to question any incident where your perceptions are negative and remind yourself of your tendencies. Check your thinking to see whether your mind is doing one of the Belief Keepers of Mind Reading, Selective Perception, Exclusion Delusion, or Blame Magnet. You may also need to review the chapters on perception or the exercises in those chapters.

Your work may focus more on stopping negative thinking patterns which were created by your heart wound. This work, in particular, requires daily persistence. When you sense such thoughts are worsening, use the rubber band technique again. Use it as long as you need to. You may need to start doing the journal again. I actually recommend that you make the journal a life-long practice, regardless of how well you are doing. It helps keep you on track.

Finally, your work may focus on relationships. A wound of the heart can't heal when you are in a relationship with someone who frequently jabs that wound. You may need to set boundaries with that person, being assertive about those behaviors you can no longer tolerate. You may need to end a relationship. In making this decision, you have to compare the pain of separation with the pain of staying with the person. Ask yourself what you would want a loved friend or your child to do in the same relationship.

The following exercise is designed to summarize much of your work in this book. Complete each statement as instructed. After you finish, read it over to yourself. Read it again. Use this summary as an anchor in your work. Let it be a reminder to you.

My hope is that your life will be more peaceful and satisfying because you realize your strengths and your intrinsic worth. My wish is that you will give yourself the same kindness, understanding, and compassion that you give to others.

My Wound of the Heart:

1. I was born a perfectly normal, loveable, intelligent, and precious baby, just like every other baby. Like every other baby, I was helpless and totally dependent on the adults around me for everything.

2. When I was a child, some bad events happened to me that made me feel as if I was not good enough or loveable enough. These events included the following: (Copy your answers to Part A in Stupid Little Girl Story. Add other events that you have recalled while working through this book.)

   _____

   _____

   _____

   _____

   _____

   _____

   _____

   _____

   _____

   _____

   _____

   _____

   _____

   _____

   _____

   _____

   _____

3. The truth is that these events were not my fault, but as a child I couldn't know this. So, I accepted the following inaccurate beliefs about myself: (Copy your answers to Part B in Stupid Little Girl Story. Add other negative

self-beliefs you have discovered as you worked through this book.)

----

4. Because I believed these false beliefs to be true, I have said many negative things to myself in my mind. These are some of the negative things I have thought to myself through the years (Copy your answers from Part C in Stupid Little Girl Story. Add others you have noted while working through the book.)

----

5. My negative beliefs about myself and how I fit into the world have sometimes caused me to make choices that have turned out to be bad for me. Some of these have been the following:

    _____

    _____

    _____

    _____

    _____

    _____

    _____

    _____

    _____

6. I now know that my childhood events were not my fault. No child deserves to be made to feel inadequate, not good enough, unimportant, or unlovable. I was a child, so I did not deserve to feel any of those things. These are the truth statements about me. (Write a truth statement for each of the false negative beliefs in # 3.)

    _____

    _____

    _____

    _____

    _____

    _____

    _____

    _____

    _____

    _____

    _____

    _____

    _____

7. Now that I know these truths, I also know that:
   A. I am equal to every other human being.
   B. I am not defective, unlovable or incompetent in any way.
   C. I can feel love and compassion for myself as well as for others.
   D. I have the power to change my life for the better.
   E. I will no longer feel shame or embarrassment for the bad things that happened to me or where I came from, as I was an innocent victim.
   F. I can live my life independent of the good opinion of others.
   G. I can be assertive about my needs and desires.
   H. I deserve to be in relationships where I am treated with love and respect.

Appendices

Appendix A
The Belief Keepers

Below you will find handouts that I give to my patients in therapy and use in my self-esteem workshops. These pages are designed to help you gain a better understanding of the Belief Keepers and to give you some techniques to combat their negative effects.

On page 202, examples of statements made to support the Belief Keepers are provided. On page 203, possible interventions are provided for each Belief Keeper.

BELIEF KEEPERS

The Exclusion Delusion: The rules that apply to every other human being don't apply to you.

a. I should have known better.
b. I should have been stronger.
c. It was different with me.
d. I can't be too easy on myself.

Emotional Compass: You listen to your feelings as a guide for your reality.

a. I just feel like....
b. I feel like a loser.
c. I have a gut sense that...
d. I can feel their rejection.

Mind Reading: You think you know what others are thinking, even though you can't actually read their minds.

a. They think that I'm...
b. He didn't like me.
c. She didn't like....
d. They aren't like me.

Selective Attention: You pay attention to the events that seem to support your beliefs, while ignoring events that contradict those beliefs.

a. I can't do anything right.
b. I mess up everything.
c. He didn't like any of my work.
d. No one cares about me.

The Blame Magnet: You find a way to blame yourself for every bad or negative event in life.

a. It was my fault.
b. Now, I've messed everything up.
c. Where did I go wrong?
d. If it hadn't been for me,....

BELIEF KEEPERS
Interventions

1. ***The Exclusion Delusion:*** The rules that apply to every other human being don't apply to me.
   Intervention: Put someone else in your shoes. Imagine someone you like and respect experienced your situation, with all the same circumstances. Imagine that they told you they were feeling what you are feeling. How would you judge them? What would you think about them? What would you say to them? You should judge yourself equally. Don't be any harder or any easier on yourself.

2. ***Emotional Compass:*** You listen to your feelings as a guide for your reality.
   Intervention: Remember that your feelings can be deceptive. In order to determine the truth of a situation, you have to rely only on the facts. Do the facts confirm your conclusion? What are the actual facts? Emotions always follow your prior negative beliefs. Don't trust them when they do.

3. ***Mind Reading:*** You think you know what others are thinking, even though you can't actually read their minds.
   Intervention: You can't actually read anyone's mind. Any assumptions you make about other's thoughts or feelings will be influenced by your prior negative beliefs. The correct answer is, "I don't know what they are thinking."

4. ***Selective Attention:*** You pay attention to the events that seem to support your beliefs, while ignoring events that contradict those beliefs.
   Intervention: To combat this tendency, you have to remind yourself of events that contradict your negative beliefs. If you attend to failures, remind yourself of successes. If you attend to people who have rejected you, remind yourself of people who care about you.

5.   ***The Blame Magnet:*** You find a way to blame yourself for every bad or negative event in life.

Intervention: To combat this tendency, you have to look for possible causes of a negative event other than your mistakes or faults. Are there other factors that could have contributed to the negative outcome? Did others play a part? Did you really have control of the situation?

Appendix B
Heart Attacks

(Thoughts that Attack Your Wound of the Heart)

Below you will find examples of negative thoughts that contribute to your wound of the heart. Each time you have one of these thoughts, you attack your heart. You worsen your heart wound.

I think you will find that these thought statements are a reflection of your negative beliefs about yourself. You will probably find that the thoughts are similar to messages that were conveyed to you during childhood. They could, however, be a reflection of messages conveyed in adulthood.

The statements are grouped into two negative belief categories, person and performance. The person category involves the belief that you are not important, valuable, or loveable. The performance category involves the belief that you are not smart, capable, or adequate.

<u>Person Oriented Negative Thoughts</u>

These thoughts stem from the belief that there is something wrong with you as a person. You don't question your abilities as much as you question your importance or worth. Person oriented negative thoughts occur when you experience a parent or caretaker who is distant, uninvolved, or non-affectionate. You may have experienced rejection from parents, other family, or peers. Those events create a heart wound that says you are lacking as a person.

- I'm not important.
- I'm not loveable.
- Others don't care about me.
- Others don't like me.
- Everyone hates me.
- Nobody cares about me.
- They're just saying that to be nice.
- People say nice things to butter you up.
- They think I'm an idiot.
- I know the real reason they didn't invite me.
- Most people don't like me.
- I think they're laughing at me.
- I think he's mad at me, or he would have called.
- I know I won't get the job.
- I'll have a miserable time at the party.
- He's going to break up with me.
- I'm such a loser.
- I'm boring.
- I have a gut feeling that he'll leave me.
- I should be more outgoing.
- I wish I could be more like her.
- It's because of me, isn't it?

Performance Oriented Negative Thoughts:

These thoughts stem from the belief that there is something wrong with your abilities. You don't question your worth or value as much as you question your competence. Such thoughts occur when you experience a parent or caretaker who is critical, demanding, or judgmental. You may have experienced events in school or in sports that made you feel inadequate or incompetent. Those events create a heart wound that says that you are lacking in ability or strengths.

- I have to make an A.
- If it's not perfect, it's wrong.
- I mess up all the time.
- I can't handle it if I strike out.
- I don't do anything right.
- Nothing works out for me.
- I have to win, or I'm nothing.
- Others say I have talent, but I don't see it.
- I guess I just lucked up.
- That must have been an easy test.
- Anybody can do what I do.
- She didn't like my presentation.
- I'm afraid I'll fail.
- I'd trade my abilities for yours any day.
- I'm a failure.
- What did I do wrong as a parent?
- I'm not smart enough to do college.
- That was a stupid mistake.
- I'm sure they thought my idea was dumb.
- I can never please them.
- All I ever do is mess up.

Appendix C
My Heart Journal

On page 209, you will find a structured form you can use for your daily journal. Simply make copies of the page for each day. Use of the form will help you gain maximum benefit from the journaling process.

1. After writing the date, you will make notes of the events of that day. You need to include any events that had an impact on your mood, self-esteem, or relationships. Some events will be big, such as an argument with a friend or spouse. Some events will seem minor, such as running five minutes late for an appointment. If a minor event had an impact on your well-being, it should be included.

    You should include external events and internal events. Internal events are thoughts you noticed during the day. You may have been affected by certain thoughts, even though no actual external event occurred.

    You should also include positive and negative events. You may have experienced an event that improved your mood or self-esteem. Definitely, include such events in the journal.

2. Next you will record your reactions to the events you recorded above. As you will note, the journal asks for actions, thoughts and feelings/emotions. Try to write something in each section. Actions will include any behaviors you did in response to the event. In the thoughts section, you should write any statements you made in your mind, in response to the event. Write down those thoughts exactly as you thought them. Don't summarize or "clean them up." If your thought was "I'm a stupid idiot," you shouldn't write, "I put myself down." In the feelings section, try to write down as many emotions as you experienced.

An event may have made you feel sad, angry, and unimportant. Write them all down.

3. The next section asks you to connect your negative behaviors, thoughts, and emotions to your negative beliefs about yourself. You will need to look back at section B in the "Story of the Stupid Little Girl" exercises. There, you wrote down ten negative beliefs that could have come from your childhood experiences. If you have reactions that don't seem to fit with one of the ten original negative beliefs, you may need to identify an additional belief about yourself that you missed in the original exercise. You can add that to the list in section B of the "Stupid Girl" story. The idea here is to make the connection between your negative thinking and your beliefs about yourself.

4. This section asks you to be your own therapist. In this section, you should think about healthy, rational, truthful, and compassionate responses to the events of that day. One way to do this is to ask yourself what you would say or think about a good friend who experienced the same event. Show the same kindness to yourself that you would show to your friend.

My Heart Journal

Today's date: _____

Events of Today: _____
_____
_____
_____
_____
_____
_____
_____

My Reactions to Those Events:

Actions: _____
_____

Thoughts: _____
_____

Feelings/Emotions: _____
_____

My reactions to these events are influenced by my beliefs about myself and the world. The beliefs impacting my reactions of today are the following:
_____
_____

My healthy, rational or wise response to today:
_____
_____
_____

Appendix D
Rubber band aid for Your Heart Wound

This is a thought stopping technique, a deceptively simple intervention that can be quite effective. Sometimes, we can identify certain thoughts or patterns of thoughts that have been hurting us. Even though we realize that those thoughts are self-destructive, we may have difficulty stopping them from coming into our minds. The thoughts seem to be a bad habit which we cannot break. The technique is designed to make you more aware of the thoughts and to stop them.

Place an ordinary rubber band on your wrist. Wear it all your waking hours. Monitor your thoughts. Any time you notice yourself having a negative thought about yourself, pop the rubber band. Don't pull it back very far. The point isn't to cause pain. You just flip it lightly and think to yourself, "I did it again." Continue on with your day, but continue monitoring your thoughts. The next time you notice a negative thought about yourself, repeat the procedure.

Sometimes, my clients report that people have questioned them about why they are wearing a rubber band on their wrist. I remind them that they are wearing it to get rid of negative beliefs or thoughts that wounded them as a child. I remind them that the wounded little girl or little boy is still within them (the inner child), and that their negative thoughts or beliefs continue to hurt that child. I then recommend that they respond, when questioned, that they are wearing the rubber band at the request of a little girl or a little boy and that they don't want to let them down.

The first three or four days you do this technique, you will become more aware of how frequently you have negative self-talk. After several days, you will begin to think of the negative statements differently. The thoughts will begin to feel like a bad habit rather than reality. You will begin to listen to the thoughts less. The frequency of the thoughts will gradually decrease. Do this technique every day for a month. See how it works!

About the Author

Terry L. Ledford, Ph.D. has been in private practice for over thirty years at Woodridge Psychological Associates. Prior to that, he served as Director of Adult Services for Rutherford/Polk Mental Health Center and taught psychology at Alfred University in New York. After receiving his doctorate from the University of Georgia, he completed post-doctoral training in Strategic Family Therapy and Cognitive/Behavioral Therapy. His psychotherapy techniques have been shaped by that training. Through the years Dr. Ledford developed a treatment approach that incorporates the emotional connection of the therapeutic story with the logical appeal of cognitive therapy. This blending of techniques helps his clients by appealing to the rational mind and their emotional mind (i.e. the head and the heart). He currently lives with his wife in the mountains of western North Carolina.

Made in the USA
Lexington, KY
26 April 2016